THE
THREE-LEGGED
STOOL

Employee Engagement = Higher Profits

DANA COUILLARD

◆ FriesenPress

Suite 300 - 990 Fort St
Victoria, BC, V8V 3K2
Canada

www.friesenpress.com

Copyright © 2020 by Dana Couillard
First Edition — 2020

Author Photograph by Rob Olson Photography

ISBN
978-1-5255-5520-6 (Hardcover)
978-1-5255-5521-3 (Paperback)
978-1-5255-5522-0 (eBook)

1. BUSINESS & ECONOMICS, CORPORATE FINANCE
2. BUSINESS & ECONOMICS, MENTORING & COACHING
3. BUSINESS & ECONOMICS, LEADERSHIP

Distributed to the trade by The Ingram Book Company

TABLE OF CONTENTS

This book is dedicated to my mother, Terri, and my late father, Judd, who were business people at heart their entire working lives. They instilled the excitement of being a business owner in each of their four sons throughout our careers.

Mom, at 90, you are still an inspiration to our entire family.

INTRODUCTION

In *Breakfast at the Victory*, James Carse provides a great parable that symbolizes the impact of perception on a group of people who are experiencing the same event.

> One morning, the master said to his students that they would walk to the top of the mountain. The students were surprised because even those who had been with him for years thought the master was oblivious to the mountain whose crest looked serenely on their town.
>
> By midday, it became apparent that the master had lost direction. Moreover, no provision had been made for food. There was increasing grumbling, but he continued walking, sometimes through underbrush and sometimes across faces of crumbling rock.
>
> When they reached the summit in the late afternoon, they found other wanderers already there who had strolled up a well-worn path. When the students complained to the master, he said only, "These others had climbed a different mountain."

One of the first things I am asked as a business mentor and coach is "Where do I start?" Much like the trip up the mountain, the answer to that question is as unique as the people who ask it. It depends on your perception and purpose for making the journey.

The Three-Legged Stool is a powerful new tool designed to help business leaders harness the power of profitability through purpose and employee engagement. In my more than twenty years as a business behaviour mentor, I have found five observations to be true.

First, the greater the awareness of all aspects of the current climate and culture of an organization, the better. You can't build on strengths or work on challenges unless you know what they are.

Second, the employees on the front lines tend to have the most enlightening information because they are usually closest to the work and, often, the customer.

Third, the best way to both immediately increase engagement and gather this information is to have open dialogues based on specific questions with as many employees and supervisors as possible.

Fourth, execution of the entire initiative is absolutely critical. Action must not only be perceived as happening, employees actually need to see and feel its impact.

Fifth, high employee engagement is absolutely critical in order for a company to effectively meet customers' needs and to maintain a stable growth profile.

Consider the following two questions about your business or organization.

1. **Would you like to know how much low employee engagement is costing your organization and what to do about it?**
2. **Besides making a profit, why does your company do what it does?**

The Three-Legged Stool is a business leader's road map for the journey to higher employee engagement. I have used a variety of stories from my own writing and research for this book, along with interviews with business leaders, and experiences with many clients over the years. I've included these stories to challenge your current thinking and help you understand and relate to the key concepts in this book.

Purpose is an action, not just a word. Throughout the book, you will be challenged to think in different ways and to have more meaningful discussions with your managers, employees, shareholders, and customers. Most of the answers we seek are inside us already. This is the heartland of starting to enhance employee engagement.

You will be challenged to:

- Identify and manage Public Enemy #1 in your business.
- Apply the power of the psychological needs of purpose, control, competence, and connection to your organization.
- Create and utilize your own unique purpose statement to lead your organization into the future.

Arthur Ashe was the first African American to win the men's singles at Wimbledon and the US Open, and the first African American man to be ranked number one in the world. He is quoted as saying: "Success is a journey, not a destination. The doing is often more important than the outcome." I hope you enjoy your journey, your doing!

1

THE SHIP THAT WOULDN'T DIE

On the morning of April 16, 1945, twenty-two Japanese kamikaze planes attacked the *USS Laffey*, a battle destroyer on observation duty on the front lines of the Pacific sea battle. The *Laffey* was alone with no sea or air support at the time and fighting for its life. The battle lasted only eighty minutes!

In *Hell from the Heavens, the Epic Story of the USS Laffey and World War II's Greatest Kamikaze Attack,* John Wukovitz tells the story of what the US Navy described as "one of the great sea epics of war."[1] It became known as the ship that wouldn't die.

Imagine being in those gun turrets with the feeling that each kamikaze pilot was coming right at you! Imagine the fear in your throat and the way your heart would race. Each man had to know precisely what he was trained to do as part of the overall operation of the ship.

After the first twelve kamikazes, Quartermaster Ari Phoutrides was sent from the bridge to survey the damage. He delivered a sobering report:

> *Both the main deck and the superstructure deck aft, upon which rested many of the ship's guns, were a mass of flames. Enemy planes, bombs, machine gun fire, and shrapnel had punctured holes in the decks ranging from inches to several feet in diameter. The fantail [the back of the ship] was all the way down in the water and still going down further. Engines and aircraft pieces protruded from gun mounts and below-deck compartments, and every rear gun had been destroyed or badly damaged. Smoke billowed skyward, while flames*

on deck and flooding below decks threatened to scuttle the Laffey *before additional kamikazes even had the chance. The radar was gone and the rudder was jammed so that the ship could only travel in a circle, its only evasive technique being either to speed up or slow down.*[2]

And the battle was only half over! Through all of this, working together, they survived the attacks of ten more kamikaze planes before support arrived.

The aftermath? Twenty-two Japanese pilots were shot down or died crashing their plane into the ship. With thirty-two deaths and seventy wounded among its crew and shrouded in smoke and fire for hours, "the *Laffey* somehow survived, and the gutted American warship limped from Okinawa's shore for home, where the ship and crew would be feted as heroes."[3]

The ship's skipper, Commander F. Julian Becton, was a highly trained, experienced, and decorated naval officer. He and his officers trained their men diligently and repetitively on all aspects of operating a fighting US warship.

As I read this book and learned of the hard training, comradeship, and a clear purpose that marked this ship's oversight, something occurred to me. Although "employee engagement" was probably not a term commonly used in 1945, Becton had hit all of the hallmarks of a highly engaged crew. Let's take a look.

CONTROL & EMPOWERMENT

Becton believed in empowering all of his officers to do what they needed to. Rather than micromanage every detail, Becton described what he wanted done, and then trusted the men to accomplish it. *"Now go ahead and do it,"* Becton would say. *"I assume you can do it. Let me know if you have any trouble, but otherwise it's yours."*[4] He put his trust in his men, knowing that a high level of trust was critical to the process.

As part of this empowerment, Becton continually checked to make certain each department had what it needed to operate efficiently and questioned each officer to ensure he fully understood his duties. It would appear that Becton intuitively knew that part of the control process was making sure that each crew member had the resources to do his job.

COMPETENCE & MASTERY

Becton and his officers worked relentlessly on competencies and skills. These were the backbone every crew member needed to be able to meet and exceed their expectations under fire. He wanted his men to achieve peak efficiency and competency in all areas. They worked on search-and-destroy drills, towing exercises, smoke laying, nighttime attacks, and shell handling, and conducted gunnery practice for the 20mm, 40mm and five-inch guns on deck. Teamwork required all crew to be at their fighting best in the individual jobs they had as part of the overall operation of the destroyer.

Every time a blip on the radar occurred or a lookout spotted something unusual on the endless flat horizon, there would be a General Call to Quarters. This meant that all men had to go to their battle stations as fast as humanly possible within the narrow confines of the ship. This happened repetitively, day and night, while in the battle zone, sometimes resulting in battle, many times not.

CONNECTION & BELONGING

The crew on the *Laffey* lived and operated in extremely close quarters. Efficient movement and operations were required by all. Every sailor knew his team—he had to—his life and the lives of his teammates depended on it. There was a sense among the men that they belonged on the ship and that they could count on their teammates and the rest of their crew. Each crew member felt a connection to something bigger than themselves: their crew, their ship, winning the war.

PURPOSE & MEANING

The crew of the *USS Laffey* was probably like any other crew, a cross-section of men of different ages, experiences, religious backgrounds, training, and cultures. But they had an overriding purpose that bonded them together:

the defense of their country. On that April morning, "each nudged aside the differences and the dangers and nobly served their skipper, and their ship mates."[5] Young men just out of high school manned their 20 mm guns and fired them at low-level kamikazes flying directly at them. Executive officer, Lieutenant McCune, said of them later, "You know, some of those kids have more damned guts—they stayed right in that gun mount and kept firing."[6] They also died in their mounts. These men had guts that were guided by a deep sense of purpose and commitment!

It is the role of the leaders of an organization to identify, clarify, and live the purpose of the organization. Like the purpose felt by the crew of the *Laffey*, the purpose of any organization should go beyond its bounds. It should be a commitment to a greater good, to community, to making the world a better place *because* of its business.

LEADERSHIP & ENGAGEMENT

On the *USS Laffey*, all of these aspects of engagement started at the top with Commander Becton. He was the one who was in charge of his officers who trained their crews relentlessly in preparation for battle (*competence*). He was the one who empowered them to do what they needed to do and made sure they had the resources to support it (*control*). He was the one who unified his men around the defense of their ship and their country (*purpose*). He was the one who inspired each officer, who in turn inspired the men below them, to function as a highly efficient naval war machine (*connection*).

2

DOING BUSINESS ON A THREE-LEGGED STOOL

Have you ever sat at a wobbly four-legged table and one of the legs doesn't touch the uneven floor? Have you ever sat on a four-legged chair that wobbled annoyingly every time you moved or shifted your weight?

Whenever the chair or table wobbled, it would find stability on the three remaining legs that were still touching the floor. If either one wobbled back again, it would be another combination of three legs that stabilized the rocking. Any combination of three legs provided stability until you shifted your weight on the chair or leaned differently on the table. Of course, we could temporarily fix this by folding up a napkin or drink coaster and wedging it under whichever leg was not touching the floor at that time.

As you no doubt have figured out by now, it takes a minimum of three legs to make the table or the chair balance properly on uneven floors. It is this mathematical certainty that creates the power of a three-legged stool – the power of stability and equilibrium.

I have chosen the metaphor of a three-legged stool to illustrate the interaction of the four fundamental needs illustrated in the story of the ship that wouldn't die.

The three-legged stool illustrates how purpose, control, competence, and connection are tied together. One leg represents control, one represents competence, and one represents connection. The seat of the stool represents purpose, the need that ties the three legs together. Regardless of the surface it's set on, a three-legged stool will always be balanced. By managing all four parts of the stool (purpose, control, competence, and connection), organizations can navigate the peaks and valleys of doing business, knowing they can maintain their balance.

This three-legged stool represents self- or internal motivation. All four aspects of the stool are necessary to have the highest levels of self-motivation. The opposite form of motivation is external motivation that comes from your environment and not from within. Self-motivation means you make decisions and take actions because you want to, based on who you are. Internal and external motivation are opposite ends of a continuum and individuals can experience different types of motivation in different situations.

The four psychological needs of purpose, control, competence and connection are as essential to mental well-being as air, water, food, and shelter are to physical well-being. When they are not supported, employee wellness begins to deteriorate, and physical and mental symptoms make appearances. Enter lower employee engagement, along with weaker performance, reduced productivity, and lower profitability.

Low employee engagement is endemic to businesses and organizations around the world. Why do I say "around the world"? Because the four basic psychological needs that are critical to employee engagement are the same four that are essential to physical, emotional, and mental wellness for all human beings. Springing from decades of work by Edward Deci and Richard Ryan on self-determination theory, the four basic needs are unbounded by culture, race, gender, personality, religion or temperament. They can impact any human being at any point in their work or personal lives.

Employees want to be put in roles that leverage their skills and abilities (strengths) and allow them to do what they do best. They want to have the tools, technology, information, and other resources they need to be effective. They don't want leaders to introduce procedural barriers that interfere with their ability to get things done. They don't want leaders to dilute their focus and consume their energy with tasks that don't add value. Finally, they want leaders to get out of the way!

Howard Schulz of Starbucks fame said, "When you're surrounded by people who share a passionate commitment around a common purpose, anything is possible." Sounds like what was going on during the the *USS Laffey*'s eighty-minute struggle for survival. There was no time for micro-managing or second guessing. Commander Becton led with the full knowledge that his team was prepared. This allowed him to focus on his main role: applying his training and experience to making critical decisions each time the *Laffey* was attacked or suffered performance-debilitating damage or human injury. He had all four fundamental parts of the three-legged stool in full play on the open ocean amongst twenty-two enemy kamikaze planes—and survived!

SOMETHING TO CONSIDER

A well-constructed three-legged stool is actually an asset to your business. In fact, it should be considered the primary asset of any business because it relates directly to physical assets: money, equipment, buildings, and inventory. If only the physical assets are planned for in a succession plan for the next generation, a key psychological asset could be left behind. In any type of succession planning, processes for continuing to measure and manage employee engagement on the three-legged stool are absolutely critical.

SO NOW WHAT?

1. What is your role in increasing employee engagement in your organization?
2. Is the overriding sense of purpose and commitment flowing from the executive offices to the front-line employees?
3. Has your purpose been clearly communicated to your customers in order to engage them at a deeper emotional level?
4. Have you included the three-legged stool or employment engagement as an asset in your succession plan?

3

THIS THING CALLED EMPLOYEE ENGAGEMENT

Lisa Osachoff, senior vice-president of people and culture of the Western Financial Group, told me, "Employee engagement to me is really the measure of the overall employee experience. Employee experience is the way in which individuals in organizations feel about their work, their peers, their direct and indirect leaders, and the organization overall."

"What is important to note about employee engagement is that there are usually other layers within the metric itself that will help build out an action plan or road map of how to impact the employee experience. To me, employee engagement represents how an employee feels about your overall organization as a brand and as an employer."

She had shared with me a copy of a graphic outlining the Western Financial 2018-2020 Strategy. It was a series of horizontal boxes of varying sizes arranged in a pyramid format. Each box got smaller as they approached the top. The very top box contained the words "Increased Profit." Not surprisingly, the very bottom box, the box that supported the entire structure, said, "Engaged, Motivated, and Empowered People." It was a clear graphic that emphasized the power of employee engagement!

During an interview with Scott Murakami of KB Heating and Air Conditioning, he defined employee engagement "as being part of a team, feeling that there is a purpose to our employees' employment. It is having a sense of satisfaction at the end of the day, knowing they play a role in the success or failure of their department or of the company." He added,

"It's important for our employees to feel respect and appreciation for their contributions."

Another related definition of employee engagement came up during my conversation with Trevor Campbell, director of the Jack Ady Cancer Centre. "Employee engagement to me means that all our staff are able to complete their tasks autonomously and have decision making ability. At Jack Ady, the frontline staff has a high degree of engagement because they are using their learning and skills every day."

You can see all four parts of the three-legged stool hidden in the definitions above: control and competence in Trevor's description, connection in Lisa's description, purpose and connection in Scott's definition. As I have discussed, high employee engagement requires high levels of feelings of purpose, control, competence, and connection in any organization. As former Campbell's Soup CEO, Doug Conant, once said, "To win in the marketplace you must first win in the workplace." Employee engagement is the key to activating a high performing workforce.

Highly engaged organizations make money by making a difference in the lives of all their employees, customers, vendors, investors and the communities they serve. Engaged leaders create and build the kinds of companies that employees want to work for, that investors respect and invest in, that customers come back to time after time, and that communities welcome into their midst.

Employee engagement is the extent to which employees feel passionate about their jobs, are committed to the organization, and put discretionary effort into their work. It is not the same as employee satisfaction. Satisfaction only indicates how happy or content your employees are. It does not measure their emotional commitment or their level of motivation or involvement. An employee's satisfaction score could be high because they are satisfied with collecting a paycheck while doing as little work as possible. This could be somewhat misleading as a measure of true employee engagement. That particular employee could be described as an unengaged employee.

You've heard the management adage, "If it can be measured, it can be managed." The good news is that employee engagement as it relates to the four fundamental psychological needs can be both measured *and* managed.

It is a business strategy that will start increasing engagement, from the first day that you seriously start to explore the concept in your business.

How can I be so sure? Because in every organization I've worked with, without exception, the moment we start talking about engagement the conversation takes on a new meaning, a new sense of importance and pending excitement. That is the first sign of engagement, the first spark from the fire that burns beneath the surface. It is the spark that can be fanned into the flames of an enhanced business culture and a new sense of meaning and purpose for leaders, employees, shareholders, and, most importantly, customers.

Osachoff at Western Financial believes that "employee engagement as a measure is as important as any financial metric for success. We've taken on some transformational efforts at Western over the last few years. Change is hard and can, although not always, impact employee engagement. We are just now set to really start to capitalize and build on the foundational elements of a solid base of employee engagement."

When asked if they had a process for measuring and monitoring employee engagement, Campbell at the Jack Ady Centre indicated that "[our organization] completes the *Our People Survey* every two years. Part of the survey has questions that specifically focus on certain characteristics of employee engagement." Their organization believes measuring employee engagement is a key metric to understanding and enhancing overall performance.

Ken Blanchard is quoted as saying, "Connect the dots between individual roles and the goals of the organization. When people see that connection, they get a lot of energy out of work. They feel the importance, dignity, and meaning in their job."

When all four core needs–purpose, control, competence, and connection–are in place, what does employee engagement really look like? Without knowing what the characteristics of the various levels of employee engagement are, trying to achieve higher engagement might be akin to building a puzzle without the picture on the lid. The following chapter will help you discover the different pieces of the puzzle!

SO NOW WHAT?

1. How do you define employee engagement for your organization?
2. How do you regularly and consistently measure employee engagement in your company?
3. What is the current engagement level of your employees?

4

WHAT EMPLOYEE ENGAGEMENT LOOKS LIKE

So, what does engagement look like? Employee engagement is usually divided into three categories: **engaged** employees, **unengaged** employees, and **actively disengaged** employees. No doubt you will recognize some of your employees in each set of characteristics.

ENGAGED EMPLOYEES

According to a 2018 report from the Canadian Human Resources Centre,[1] engaged employees represent only 25 percent of the workforce, about one in four employees. Engaged employees:

- have high levels of enthusiasm;
- are motivated and self-starters;
- are satisfied and happy with their careers;
- believe in, and are loyal to, the organization;
- are focused and keen to take on challenges;
- have a problem-solving attitude;
- have high overall work performance;
- are committed and take responsibility;
- care about long-term success;
- are willing to help out wherever they can;
- create a positive environment;
- have positive mental and physical well-being.

UNENGAGED EMPLOYEES

In contrast to engaged employees, unengaged employees represent a huge 60 percent of the workforce.[2] These employees:

- punch the clock, sleepwalk through their days, and generally just aren't there;
- are psychologically unattached to their work and company;
- are very difficult to spot in the workplace;
- are indifferent and neither like nor dislike their job;
- represent a risk—a risk that can tilt positively or negatively;
- want to be inspired but are currently uninspired—they need an extra push to perform at their best;
- are putting time but not energy or passion into their work because their needs aren't being met;
- have high levels of presenteeism (being present at work but being relatively unproductive).

ACTIVELY DISENGAGED EMPLOYEES

Actively disengaged employees are in a league of their own. They have all of the characteristics of the unengaged employees—and more! They are as much active in a negative way as engaged employees are active in a positive way. Representing 15 percent of the workforce,[3] actively disengaged employees:

- aren't just unhappy at work, they are resentful that their needs aren't being met;
- are spreaders of doom and gloom to demonstrate how unhappy they are;
- are busy acting out their unhappiness;
- undermine or damage every day what their engaged co-workers accomplish;
- spread toxic mistrust and doubt in the organization's management and the company's future;
- have high levels of presenteeism or absenteeism.

What is the cost of low engagement? Statistics show that unhappy workers cost the North American business economy an estimated $450 billion to $550 billion US per year in lost productivity.[4] These are costs that go largely unidentified by many businesses and directly impact the bottom line. They are also costs that can be recovered when a company identifies its core purpose and focuses on creating a supportive environment for employee control, competency, and connection.

According to the Industrial Accident Prevention Association of Canada,[5] the costs of doing nothing can be staggering. Some in the list below tend to be indirect costs, costs that are difficult to measure. Those are the costs that result from the insidious impact of low engagement and poor mental health.

- Increased employee turnover
- Increased health insurance claims
- Decreased employee satisfaction
- Increased short- & long-term disability
- Lower employee engagement
- Increased depression
- Increased absenteeism
- Increased accidents
- Higher presenteeism
- Reduced productivity
- Lower customer ratings
- Higher operating costs

There are also compounding costs that quite often are the result of high stress and low mental wellness.[6] Compared to an average group of employees, these employees can have:

- 3 times risk of heart problems
- 2-3 times mental health problems
- 2 times substance abuse
- 2-3 times conflicts
- 2-3 times injuries
- 5 times certain cancers
- 2-3 times infections
- 3 times back pain

I have developed a simple calculator to calculate the potential losses of low engagement in your organization. The calculations are based on the latest research and statistics as of the writing of this book. You can access your free PDF version of *Calculating The Potential Costs of Low Employee Engagement* at my business website www.rippledynamics.com.

I use the word "losses" hesitantly because, in actual fact, the numbers you arrive at represent potential opportunities to improve employee wellness and engagement, productivity, and profitability. Take the time to do these quick calculations—you'll be surprised at what you discover about your business.

Approaching engagement as a business strategy clearly yields improved results. When businesses in the top 25 percent of the 2016 Gallup State of the American Workplace Study[7] employed employee engagement improvement strategies, they showed the following improvement in results vs businesses in the bottom 25 percent.

- 20% higher sales
- 21% increase in profitability
- 41% decrease in absenteeism
- 70% fewer employee safety incidents
- 17% higher productivity

- 24% lower turnover in high turnover organizations
- 59% lower turnover in low-turnover organizations
- 28% less shrinkage or theft
- 10% higher in customer satisfaction & retention
- 40% decrease in quality defects

A CAUTIONARY NOTE

Not all employees in any given business or organization may be engaged. In fact, some may resist attempts at becoming more engaged in the work place. This can happen for a variety of reasons, some personal to the individual and some intrinsic within the organization. At some point, leaders in the organization may just toss up their hands and wonder what to do with a very unengaged or actively disengaged employee.

Sometimes this can be avoided during the selection process. Scott Murakami of KB Heating and Air Conditioning said, "We try to differentiate between a good employee and a good tradesman. We can usually teach a good employee to be a good tradesman, but we can't teach a good tradesman to be a good employee. To us, a good employee is much more valuable than a good tradesman.

"When evaluating an employee, we ask our managers to ask themselves: 'Is this the type of person you want to build your department around?' If the answer is no, it may be time to replace that person. By keeping him or her, it means that there's one less spot for someone that may show much more potential. They are occupying a seat on the bus that is preventing someone else much more deserving from using it."

Jim Collins, in *Good to Great*, says it is imperative for every business to get the right people on the bus. It is also important to get the right people in the right seats once they are on the bus. Some organizations have the capacity to try to retrain or reposition unengaged or disengaged employees within the organization. In reality, some employees may not be able to find a seat on the bus. They may even be on the wrong bus, taking up valuable space. In cases like this, I believe business leaders have to make the tough call to let those employees go. It is time to ask them to leave the bus altogether.

Jim Sinegal, co-founder and former CEO of Costco, once said, "When your employees are happy, they are your very best ambassadors." Andrew Carnegie, an industrialist, business magnate, and philanthropist in the early part of the twentieth century, said, "The average person puts only 25 percent of his energy and ability into his work. The world takes off its hat to those who put in more than 50 percent of their capacity and stands on its head for those few and far between souls who devote 100 percent." His descriptors of the different levels of employee engagement are almost 100 years old. Do you see any similarity to today?

SO NOW WHAT?

1. What is the potential cost of doing nothing to increase employee engagement in your organization? To get your free copy of *Calculating The Potential costs of Low Employee Engagement*, go to www.rippledynamics.com.

2. What are the potential gains for your organization? Use some of the percentage data from the Gallup study above for your calculations.
3. What is the one thing you can take from this chapter and immediately act upon?

5

PUBLIC ENEMY #1

Since its inception, the FBI has listed over 500 fugitives on their most-wanted list. The first man to be number one was thin, perhaps about 160-170 pounds, around 5'9", and had a slightly receding head of thick, dark hair. Somewhat larger ears framed his elongated face, which was accented with a thin, pointed nose. There was a prominent Adam's apple pushing out from a thin neck that rose from broad, straight shoulders. Relatively speaking, he was as ordinary looking as ordinary could be. He appeared to be almost unassuming.

At first, he headed up his own gang of thieves, robbing cargo trucks or trains carrying bank deliveries and payrolls. They were constantly on the run in the US Midwest during and after the Great Depression era. He led just one of the many different gangs operating at the same time across the nation during the first half of the twentieth century. Born in 1896, by the time he was thirty, he and his gang had hijacked a truck and escaped with $1,350,000, their biggest heist to date and a fortune by any standards.

On the run and eluding capture for two years after that large robbery, he was eventually caught by the FBI and convicted in 1928. He was sentenced and incarcerated in the Leavenworth Federal Penitentiary, located just outside of Kansas City, Kansas. He escaped the legendary prison and was soon back on the run as a career criminal. Joining a new gang, one of whose members was George "Machine Gun" Kelly, he continued a run of daring daylight robberies where the gang managed two more big scores: one $4 million, the other $2.6 million. No small-time hoods here!

At one point, he joined up with the notorious Karpis-Barker Gang. For two more years this gang terrorized the grain belt of America during the "public enemy era." The exploits of gangs of criminals in the US Midwest gripped the American people and press. His gang eluded capture for two years, yet his name didn't create national large-print headlines in the nation's leading newspapers or breaking news bulletins on the national radio stations. At best, he was mentioned in local or state news where his crimes were committed, places like Minnesota, Illinois, and Kansas. He seemed to be able to operate without a lot of notoriety while continuing to rob banks, trucks, and trains seemingly at will. At best his career to this point could be referred to as unnoticed from a national perspective.

He was eventually caught and arrested again on July 7, 1932, while playing golf in Kansas City, Missouri, with some other gang members. Once again, he was sentenced to prison at Leavenworth. When he was paroled in 1947, he picked up his criminal career where it had left off, eluding capture while pulling off well-planned day-light robberies. Two years later, however, in a drunken argument with his wife in Chicago, he shot and killed her and her two brothers. The FBI now referred to him as "a menace to every man, woman, and child in America," and, on March 14, 1950, he was placed in the top spot of the newly created FBI Most Wanted List. His picture was plastered across America. It took fifteen more months to run him to ground.

Due to a tip from the public in June 1951, federal law enforcement eventually found him in Beaverton, Oregon, a lonely, down-trodden man eking out a living as a plasterer under the fake name, John McCullough. He was subsequently arrested and extradited back to Chicago. Sentenced to death, he died two years later in prison at the age of fifty-seven, before his death sentence could be executed. So ended the life of the very first man on the FBI Most Wanted List. His name was Thomas James Holden. Recognize it? Probably not!

Holden ran with some of the highest-profile criminals of his day, and yet his name usually does not come to mind when people think of Public Enemy #1. That distinction usually goes to the likes of other "famous" criminals, such as Al Capone, Clyde Barrow and Bonnie Parker, John Dillinger, Pretty Boy Floyd, Ma Barker, and Baby Face Nelson. Holden created havoc across the Midwest and yet did not achieve the long-lasting recognition of his more notorious contemporaries. For some reason, he managed to stay out of the spotlight. Perhaps he planned it that way or perhaps it was because the leaders of the gangs he ran with were already more famous: Machine Gun Kelly, Alvin Karpis, and Ma Barker.

In a career spanning more than twenty-five years, Holden was a journeyman at his criminal trade. During that time, he stole millions, almost with impunity. Except for his final crime of a triple homicide, he operated under the radar of the national eye, and thus didn't garner public recognition for his various crimes and the impact he was having on the public at large.

Another reason for this is because the other career criminals continued to receive top-of-mind reinforcement through ongoing Hollywood movies, television documentaries, magazine articles, and newspaper stories. The public continues to be both aware of, and fascinated by, their action-packed stories and exploits.

There is a Public Enemy #1 in your business. This public enemy lurks, much like Thomas Holden did, below the surface of your operations. It is continually operating in the background and only occasionally gets caught and dealt with like the thief it is.

6

PUBLIC ENEMY #1 IN YOUR BUSINESS

There is also a Public Enemy #1 in the business world. Like Thomas James Holden in the previous chapter, this enemy works relatively unnoticed and with little recognition in most companies. It robs them of employee wellness, productivity, and profitably. It hides well and is difficult to recognize in the midst of any business. Business leaders hunt for the cause of the higher costs and lost profitability in their financial records, their performance evaluations, and the processes and the procedures that they have established, but they fail to recognize this enemy.

What is this public enemy? It's name is frustration! Like Holden's career, frustration wreaks havoc while operating below the radar in organizations. When you look back to see what happened, frustration is not the first complicating factor that comes to mind. It is very difficult to recognize and pin down as the cause of low employee engagement. Frustration results in many different behaviours being displayed in the workplace, making it extremely difficult to recognize as the source of the behaviours. But, once it is identified and brought under the scrutiny of business leaders, it can no longer operate sinisterly in the shadows of the organization.

Many of the illnesses or afflictions that reduce productivity in the workplace are well-known: common colds and flus, chronic back pain, repetitive strain injury, injuries suffered on the job, high levels of stress due to work overload, lack of rest. These are examples of illnesses or injuries that can generally be noticed in the workplace. But frustration, Public Enemy #1 in the business world, remains hidden in the world of lost productivity. Like Thomas Holden, it only raises its head above the surface for short times to "rob profitability," and then it disappears into the background. Because frustration is not repeatedly identified as the cause of low productivity, it plays an unassuming role without the public recognition it should have.

Simply stated, frustration is the denial of individual fulfillment. It is a relatively common response to the human will not getting what it wants in response to the basic physical, emotional, and mental needs. But frustration in the workplace is more than simply not getting something you want. It is the inability of employees to succeed in their role due to organizational barriers that prevent them from being able to bring the bulk of their individual talents, skills, and abilities to their jobs. It may be an employee's need for control or freedom in their job that is being thwarted by a position whose roles, responsibilities, and procedures are spelled out in a very lock-step format. They may have a need for some level of freedom in how to perform their work.

It may be the inability to learn new skills and gain new experiences that would enhance their opportunity for growth in their job. An employee may be feeling like they don't belong on their team, in the organization, or maybe not even in their current job. They may feel like they're not connected and not making contributions to something bigger than themselves through their work.

Frustration, in all of its forms, is the primary cause of low employee engagement and lost productivity in the workplace. Because it operates below the radar, one of the biggest challenges in enhancing engagement in any organization is identifying which employees are engaged, which are unengaged, and which are actively disengaged. You have been given those characteristics in Chapter 4.

People can react either positively or negatively to frustration. We all have choices on how we deal with it. We can let it be a barrier and be overcome by it or we can take steps to deal with its source. The basic gut reactions to frustration are anger, withdrawal, and detachment.

Anger is the most common reaction and can take the form of verbal, mental, emotional, or, in the worst cases, physical abuse. Anger can be a very overt response and one that is readily identified in the workplace.

However, for some personalities, anger can be a very covert response, the anger that smolders inside for long periods of time and sometimes turns into an explosive outburst out of nowhere.

Withdrawal is another common negative reaction to frustration. Some people give up—they come to work, do the minimum required to perform their job, and go home at the end of the day, frustrated and unengaged, or perhaps even actively disengaged. Unlike anger, withdrawal behaviours tend to be more internal and therefore more difficult to recognize. Withdrawal over time can lead to detachment.

Detachment is a behaviour that is very difficult to identify as it usually does not present itself externally. Detachment means not having an emotional connection to work, a team, or a company. It means just going through the motions and guarding one's time as much as possible. It can lead to active disengagement. Individuals who are actively disengaged at work may take detachment to the extreme and become passive aggressive in their behaviour. That type of behaviour can sound like: "Sure, I'll do whatever you want" or "I won't volunteer any more information unless I'm asked."

When stressed or frustrated, individuals can move *away* from the source of frustration by withdrawing, hiding, and/or silencing themselves. They can also move *toward* what is frustrating them by seeking to please and appease the sources of frustration. Or they can move *against* frustration by being aggressive, trying to gain power over others, or thwarting others' perceived power over them. These three responses can be used at different times with different people in different situations. Regardless, all of them move us away from our purpose as well as the company's purpose.

There are four reasons why organizations are poorly positioned to recognize and respond to the concerns of frustrated employees.

The **first**, and usually the most obvious, is that business leaders and managers aren't asking the employees how their job is going, especially in terms of the four needs that increase employee engagement—purpose, control, competence, and connection.

The **second** is that employees may be providing feedback but business leaders can't hear them. They are not listening to the employee feedback or they aren't prioritizing it high enough.

The **third** reason is that business leaders don't want to know that their employees are frustrated. Think ostrich and sand. If they don't know about the problem, they don't have to solve it.

The **fourth** is that, in many cases, leaders and managers don't know what to do even if they did recognize the signs of frustration. Dealing with the soft-skill aspect of business can be very intimidating for many leaders. They may not have the training, skills, or personality for dealing with the causes of frustration or the behaviours that result from frustration.

One thing I would like to point out is that our first tendency may be to look at frustration in a negative light. It's important to remember that frustration of any type is a symptom, not an illness or a preferred way of being. It is a symptom of any of the four core psychological needs not being met. It is a symptom that shows up as certain types of behaviour, as you will see in the following chapters. The level of frustration will grow and spread the longer the needs are not being met.

A second key point to remember is that frustration and all of its trappings represent a myriad of opportunities for re-engagement and growth. When she was eleven years old, Marley Dias (who's now fourteen) started a book drive for books whose main characters were black girls. She had grown frustrated reading about white boys and dogs as part of her mandatory elementary school reading and so started a book drive called *#1000BlackGirlsBooks* with a goal of accumulating the titles of 1,000 books featuring black female protagonists. At the age of twelve, she won the Smithsonian Magazine's American Ingenuity Award in the Youth category. Since then, she has written her book, *Marley Dias Gets it Done: and So Can You* (Scholastic Inc, 2018). I believe one of her quotes richly describes the opportunities that frustration can produce: "Frustration is fuel that can lead to the development of an innovative and useful idea."

What opportunities are you missing in your organization?

SO NOW WHAT?

1. How are you measuring employee engagement?
2. What potential frustrations might your employees or leaders be feeling?

3. What processes do you have for reducing frustration in your organization?
4. Do you meet regularly one on one and in group settings to talk about frustrations in your workplace?

7

PURPOSE—THE SEAT OF ENGAGEMENT

So what is purpose?

Quite often, business terms like vision, mission, values, goals, and purpose are used interchangeably, which results in confusion throughout the organization. From my experience and perspective, vision is a statement that clearly identifies where you want your business to be at some point in the future. This is the *where*. A mission statement is designed to tell you what you have to do to get from today to your vision in the future. This is the *how*. Setting goals, defining strategies, and establishing measurable targets in a strategic plan outlines the actual steps that need to be executed. This is the *what*. Last in the strategic planning process is the assigning of responsibilities, the delegation of tasks, and the creation of teams. This is the *who*.

But . . . where is the *why*? What is the answer to the question 'Why does your business do what it does?' Simon Sinek, in his groundbreaking book *Start With Why, How Great Leaders Inspire Everyone to Take Action*,[1] tells us that people don't buy *what* we do, they buy *why* we do it. People want to make a connection to a company or organization that represents something bigger than making a profit. Purpose is the *why*. It is the core psychological need of all people, not just employees and leaders at work. John F. Kennedy said "Efforts and courage are not enough without purpose and direction."

Let's look back at the three-legged stool. On one leg, we can have different degrees of control in how we do our job. On the second leg, we can have a sufficient level of competency to do our job and meet the challenges that come our way. On the third leg, we can feel connections to our team and our company, feel a sense of belonging. However, without a sense of purpose tying them all together, there will still be a lack of meaning, a lack of making a significant contribution to our community or the world.

Employees want meaningful work—they want and need to be proud of their work. They want sustainable challenges and freedom to pursue them. They want a clear sense of purpose and direction. People want to read mysteries, not live them. Timely, relevant, meaningful, and truthful information is a must. It is absolutely critical when it comes to creating and living your organization's purpose statement. Employees want to know where they are going, why it matters, and how it fits their role. They want a level playing field with reciprocal caring and respect. Finally, they want to feel competent.

What distinguishes your business from your competitor? Your product or service? What if some of your competitors are in the exact same market—now what do you use? Your price? Customer service? Quality of service? Customer satisfaction? Warranty? Your values (e.g., trust, caring, integrity)? How many of these can be copied or met by your competitors? How many are already the same?

The most important and unique aspect you have in your business is your purpose. Why? Because it grows out of the values, experience, and history of all the people involved in your organization. They are both individually unique and unique as a group. This is your company's collective DNA, which determines the behaviours that all stakeholders see. Your personal purpose in life is specific to you: your personality, values, beliefs, experiences, race, gender, cultural background, faith, etc. The purpose of your business should grow out of your personal purpose in life. It should also grow out of the values & beliefs of your company and employees.

Purpose is the primary differentiator between competing businesses and organizations, and it is also the primary generator of employee and customer relationships. It is the ultimate unique sales proposition (USP)!

Purpose is making a better life for staff, customers, shareholders, and society in general. Purpose is using your strengths to serve others. It is the *why* that drives you forward. It is the belief that work serves to make a difference in a way that is meaningful to that person, that organization. Customers want to know a company's purpose. They have an internal need to help champion a cause in some way. They want to relate to what a company is doing beyond selling products and services, and making a profit.

Let me try to explain from my personal experience in karate. I have been training and instructing in Fudokan-Shotokan karate for over thirty-five years and will delve into this more in later chapters. For now, I would like to take one simple term from my training: *ikigai*. This is a traditional Japanese term that roughly translates into "reason for being." The training code that we recite at the end of each class includes five guiding principles that, in part, give us our reason for being:

1. Seek perfection of character.
2. Endeavour.
3. Be faithful.
4. Respect others.
5. Refrain from violent behaviour.

These are the values from which our reason for being, our *ikigai*, grows. They are the values that keep us focused on our purpose, our reason for training in the fundamentals of traditional karate. We learn to apply these principles to our lives to benefit others.

Everyone has a reason for living, a purpose for their existence. This is the source of value in one's life, the things that make life meaningful and worthwhile. Everyone's *ikigai* is unique to them because it is developed through their perception of their world. It can be found at the place where your talents and passions collide with the things the world needs.

In my work with a group of financial advisors over several years, we quite often come back to a seemingly difficult pair of questions: "What keeps you awake at night?" and "What gets you up in the morning?" How would you answer those two questions?

A lot depends on the current context of your life and your business or organization. When I am training hard and karate is a permeating part of my life, the answer to both these questions should be the same: training and application of karate to my personal life in helping others. If you are fully engaged in your business or career, the answer should also be the same and should be focused on the purpose and meaning of your life and organization.

It is easy to focus on the things that are going wrong that keep you awake at night, the stresses of managing your business or organization. These will no doubt be the same things that your brain grabs onto once it realizes that the night is over and the day is beginning.

Think of how much better life and business would be going if you were kept awake at night by the excitement and opportunity of what you might be able to accomplish with your purpose tomorrow or in the coming days, weeks or months. Now take it one more step. What if the first thing that woke you up in the morning was the realization that today was a new day and that you could actually accomplish something toward your purpose today?

Now take it one step further. What would it be like if you could help your employees engage with this purpose from their perspective? Remember— purpose is the seat of the three-legged stool. Sure, the seat needs the legs of control, competence, and connection to hold it up. But, without purpose, there is no direction, no *why*. Purpose trumps everything! The *ikigai* of your company is your reason for being. Realize and accept this concept and you'll be on your way to developing a highly engaged, highly functioning organization. Wouldn't it be great to go to sleep thinking about what you did with your *ikigai* that day and waking up to how can you use your *ikigai* today?

In his bestselling book, *Drive, The Surprising Truth About What Motivates Us,*[2] Dan Pink defines purpose as the yearning to do what we do in the service of something larger than ourselves. Organizations can have vision, mission, and values statements arranged nicely along their corridor walls, but without the answer to *why*, without a clear purpose statement, how do they identify the meaning and contribution to the lives of others?

Living a purpose should be messy. It should be the backdrop for all actions in the organization. In order for this to happen, a purpose statement needs to be created. The purpose statement should be brief, clear, and easy to remember. It should cut through the daily clutter and 'busyness.' It should be the filter for all decision-making and actions.

In the next chapter, you will learn more about purpose and have an opportunity to create a working purpose statement for your company.

SO NOW WHAT?

1. Do you currently have a clearly defined purpose statement that leads your company's vision?
2. Is this purpose statement clearly visible and understood throughout the organization? If yes, how do you know? If not, why not?
3. Is the overriding sense of purpose and commitment flowing from the leadership offices outward to the front-line employees? If yes, how do you know? If not, why not?

8

WHAT'S YOUR PURPOSE?

There is a line among the fragments of the Greek poet Archilochus that reads: "The fox knows many things, but the hedgehog knows one big thing." The fox tries many ways to attack and capture the hedgehog. He uses stealth to sneak up behind him and pounce on his unsuspecting prey. Just as the fox initiates his attack, the hedgehog becomes aware and initiates its best and only defence. Quick as a flash, it rolls into a ball with all of its sharp, hard spines pointing outward and all of the soft parts of its body unscathed inside this protective ball. The fox gets a sharp tweak in the snout, a mouth full of spines, or sharp pricks to its feet.

But the fox is a wily creature and not to be deterred. The next time, it lays a trap for the hedgehog, hiding downwind behind a tuft of grass or trail-side bush. It tries to use its exceptional speed to jump to catch the hedgehog before it does its one thing, rolling into its protective ball. But to no avail. The hedgehog has been practising and focusing on its one thing for so long that it has become exceptional at it. It is its primary means of survival and the hedgehog knows it.

On another day, the fox tries again, thinking the hedgehog hasn't seen this trick yet. When it attacks and the hedgehog rolls into a ball, the fox stands perfectly still, waiting for the hedgehog to think it is safe to unroll from its protective ball of spines, which it eventually does. So close, the fox pounces on the hedgehog. But the hedgehog reflexively rolls up again in the blink of an eye. The fox once again gets a feeling of the spines in its paws.

The sly fox knows of many ways to hunt many different animals to survive, and has to employ different tactics and techniques to be successful. The hedgehog has developed its one way of being successful in staying alive.

Jim Collins, in his bestselling book, *Good to Great, Why Some Companies Make the Leap . . . And Others Don't*,[1] adapts the hedgehog and fox metaphor to describe highly successful, "great" companies in comparison to merely "good" companies. "Those who built the good-to-great companies were, to one degree or another, hedgehogs. They used their hedgehog nature to drive toward what we came to call a Hedgehog Concept for their companies."

The Hedgehog Concept is a simple model to observe and a much more difficult task to implement. In its simplicity, the Hedgehog Concept is presented as three intersecting circles, each representing one of the following three fundamental questions:

1. What are you deeply passionate about?
2. What can you be the best in the world at?
3. How can I make money doing it?

The place where all three circles intersect is your Hedgehog Concept. Your goal is to identify yours, simplify it into a clear, concise concept, and let it drive everything you do. This one thing that drives everything you do has a name: purpose. As I said earlier, purpose trumps everything and drives everything. It is the ultimate filter for justifying every action your company takes on its way to enhancing employee wellness, improving productivity, and increasing profitability, all while you are making a significant contribution to the greater community.

Business purpose is the most critical factor that ties and lifts employee engagement beyond the repetitive, day-to-day culture that exists in many businesses. However, purpose without control, competence, or connection is difficult to achieve. A purpose statement provides business owners with key information that provides new perspectives of their business and work environment.

The primary goal of this chapter is to have you develop your own company purpose statement. The first thing I suggest is to do a quick and simple purpose audit. Give each employee in your organization a 5"x3" index card and have them answer one question: **"Aside from making a profit, why does this company do what it does?"**

I have done this with many companies, even some who thought they had a vision or mission statement that could act as a purpose statement. The results of this activity are generally the same. Sometimes with smaller companies, a trend or theme might emerge. But there is no high correlation between the responses. Each employees' response is unique to them. In larger companies, the range of responses tends to increase and it becomes more difficult to find a theme or trend in them.

There is a wealth of information contained in the responses to this one simple question. First, you will see that there is a wide range of answers that sometimes show a lack of understanding about what a company's purpose is. Second, some try to remember the mission or vision statement and do their best to write it down from memory. Third, the answers provide excellent jumping-off points when turned into questions. Fourth, usually a clear, concise, motivating purpose statement is not available or, if it is, it is not being communicated clearly to the all members of the company.

During World War II, passwords and countersigns were used when soldiers were returning to base following a scouting mission. For example, during the D-Day invasion, the password for the returning patrol was "flash," and the countersign by the guard was "thunder." For additional security, there was a second countersign required to complete the process by the returning patrol and it was the word "Welcome." If the process wasn't completed correctly, the incoming soldier and/or his patrol could be shot, especially in the dead dark of night. Under pressure of losing their lives, the returning soldiers and their units had to get it right the first time.

A purpose statement in any company should be that clear and that simple. Anyone in the organization should be able to state it at gunpoint. Now we know that pointing a gun at someone is not an appropriate response, but the organization's purpose should be ingrained in the work employees do, and how they interact with their team members and customers.

An effective purpose statement can follow any of three types of templates:

1. To_____(make a contribution to)_____. For example, Facebook's purpose is "to give people the power to build community and bring the world closer together." The *why* in this statement is very clear: to bring the world closer together.

2. To_____(make a contribution)_____so that _____(some type of impact occurs)_____. For example, the purpose statement of La Marzocco (a high-end Italian coffee machine manufacturer) is "to cultivate relationships so that the lives of others are enriched." The *why* in this purpose statement is also very clear: to enrich the lives of others.

3. Adam Leipzig, Hollywood director/producer, created a five-step format in his TED Talk: *How to Know Your Life's Purpose in Five Minutes.*[2] The five questions are:
    *   Who are you?
    *   What do you love to do?
    *   Who do you do it for?
    *   What do these people want or need?
    *   How are these people changed as a result?

Here is an example using Leipzig's model: When someone asks a clothing manufacturer what they do, they can respond "I help people look and feel their best. My purpose is to design apparel for men and woman who need affordable choices so they can look and feel their best."

My purpose statement for my company, Ripple Dynamics, is: *to inspire business leaders to harness the profitability of purpose and engagement.* Here are a few more examples:

*   AirBnB: To connect millions of people in real life all over the world, through a community marketplace, so that you can belong anywhere.
*   Warby Parker: A world where everyone can see clearly, stylishly, and at affordable prices.
*   Renewology (waste recycling company): To end landfilling and create a clean and secure new energy source for a more sustainable world.
*   Kellogg's: Nourishing families so they can flourish and thrive.

You will notice that, in each of these examples, the focus is outward, not inward. The focus is on making a difference in the lives of others. In doing so, we feel good about ourselves. It is very important to identify what action is being taken or what contribution is being made and why. Through my various research and readings, I have collected a variety of different purpose statements that I've included in Appendix A. I encourage you to read through them to get a sense of what these types of statements look like. You will notice that they are different from most vision or mission statements. The purpose statement must be clear, it must stand alone, and it must be integrated into every aspect of the organization.

The three questions from the hedgehog principle and the questions below will help you discover your purpose, especially if the communication and dialogue are with all members of your organization. Here are the hedgehog questions again:

1. What are you deeply passionate about?
2. What can you be the best in the world at?
3. How can you make money doing it?

The answers to these questions will help you discover the contribution you want to make. Sometimes the more difficult part of the task is to identify *why* you want to make that contribution, to clearly identify what impact it will have on the people or community that you are trying to help. However, it will come out through effective dialogue. Talk to your employees, managers, shareholders, and customers. Get to know their stories, values, and purpose. It is a great starting point but it is only the beginning of *doing* purpose, of making a clear, emotionally charged purpose statement that defines your business.

SO NOW WHAT?

1. What needs or problems exist in your community? How can you play a role and make a difference in your community?
2. How will the world be better because of your company's contributions?

3. Has your purpose been clearly communicated to your customers in order to engage them at a deeper emotional level? If yes, how do you know? If not, why not?
4. How often do you refer to your values and purpose in meetings or conversations with others in the organization?

9

CONTROL—THE FIRST LEG

In *Drive, the Surprising Truth About What Motivates Us*, Daniel Pink defines autonomy as "the urge to direct one's life."[1] Steve Jobs may have intuitively put this into motion when he said, "The people who are doing the work are the moving force behind the Macintosh. My job is to create a space for them, to clear out the rest of the organization, and keep it at bay." In the early part of the twentieth century, perhaps Booker T. Washington, who was an educator and advisor to American presidents, had anticipated this need for control when he said, "Few things can help an individual more than to place responsibility on him, and to let him know that you trust him." Notice the reference to the word "trust."

Trust is a common thread that runs through employee engagement. It is required to empower or provide control. It is a key component of building connections and relationships. It is important to allow employees to develop and explore new skills and experiences. Finally, it is a key component of instilling a sense of purpose in an organization. All people within the organization must trust that this new initiative about purpose will be fully and effectively executed, not just another fly-by-night initiative from those on high.

At work, control is the opportunity to define and improve work processes. Control fuels engagement, growth, and health because it allows people to experience themselves as the initiators of their own actions. Deadlines, imposed goals, surveillance, and many types of performance evaluations have been found to undermine self-motivation. They create frustration because they are perceived as antagonistic toward control.

They can drain an employee's sense of enthusiasm and interest in controlled activities.

Control is the ability to make a meaningful choice, which in turn engages willingness. Meaningful choice encourages people to fully endorse what they are doing. It pulls them into the activity and allows them a greater sense of willingness and engagement. Higher levels of control increase a person's self-motivation. It also increases their desire to participate and perhaps take on additional responsibilities. Sometimes, control is as simple as having the opportunity to choose—to choose how to organize your workspace, your work, even your break schedule.

But control does not mean having wide-open boundaries for the employee to do what they want. One of the key aspects of control at work is setting broad yet clear boundaries. And it's best to help employees manage their freedom within them. Once the expectations are set, the employee knows what they have to do to meet them.

Boundary setting is extremely important for promoting responsibility. Setting boundaries by encouraging input from the people who are doing the work allows them to realize that they are proactive participants. This encourages responsibility without undermining authenticity.

What do these boundaries look like? They are made up of values, sometimes the company's and sometimes the leader's. Trust is the beginning and the end point of the set of values that act as decision-making boundaries. Without trust, the very foundation of the corporation is weak.

Values should have specific behaviours attached to them so that employees know which are acceptable and which are not. This is called operationalizing the company's values. Examples of values could include trust, integrity, responsibility, commitment, respect, and caring. The first place to begin is to review your company's values. If you don't have any, this would be a great time to define a few. If you do have defined values, then work as a team to determine what behaviours each value defines.

For example, if responsibility is one of the company values, then it becomes unacceptable when a particular employee is not meeting the responsibilities in their job. This is a point when the business leader can sit down with the employee, review the behaviours that have been accepted as being responsible, and compare those to the employee's current behaviours that go against the agreed upon behaviours for responsibility.

Lee Colan, in *Engaging the Hearts and Minds of All Your Employees,* refers to the collective behaviours that correlate with each of the values as the rules of engagement—the behaviours that contribute to an engaging workplace. "These rules of engagement might address how to make decisions, share information, consider ideas for improvement, coordinate hand-offs between departments, review work, challenge prevailing thought, prioritize, or resolve conflict."[2]

There are seven key conditions that can facilitate and enhance support for control in your work place.

1. **Absence of pressure**: with an absence of pressure comes the opportunity for some control on the parameters of completing the project or getting the work done.
2. **Goal choice**: having some input into the goals that are being set provides the staff member with some degree of control, some sense that they have a say in things that have an impact on their performance.
3. **Strategy choice**: much like goal choice, it is important to include employees in the development of strategies that will have an impact on their overall work performance.
4. **Task involvement**: when responsibility for tasks is being developed and assigned, make sure that employees are involved in as much of the process as possible.
5. **Promotion of task interest and value**: employees should have some level of interest in the tasks being assigned them. They should also see value in their work, and how it aligns to overall production or operations, and the overall goals and purpose of the company.
6. **Reduced barriers/obstacles**: quite often, engaged employees bump into bureaucratic barriers that hinder their performance and their need for some control in how they can best perform their work. As Steve Jobs said, "My job is to create a space for them, to clear out the rest of the organization, and keep it at bay."
7. **Broad yet clear boundaries**: every employee wants to know the guidelines and expectations of their roles and responsibilities.

When the employee knows these, they can develop the actions and behaviours that can provide them with the most success within those boundaries.

Depending on the workplace, it may not be possible to incorporate all of the conditions. For example, in an assembly-line manufacturing company, it may be difficult to avoid the presence of pressure to some degree.

When it relates to employees having some level of control over their workplace and responsibilities, Lisa at Western Financial indicated, "Ultimately control comes hand-in-hand with the delivery of results. It's a two–way street for both the employee and the employer. An employer needs to offer a reasonable level of trust to their employees. Employees then need to deliver results. The ensuing dance of trust and control continues." She said that, in their retail offices, there are systems and processes that allow for a more efficient management of work and meeting client's needs. "We are not a highly scripted organization, so there is control in that respect."

At the Jack Ady Cancer Centre, Trevor told me that "local unit decision making is in place. We have only one focus and that is the patient. Our jobs are very directed at a goal of getting the patient through treatment." A sense of control over their jobs was providing for a higher level of self-motivation for the employees.

There are also conditions that can undermine support for control or autonomy. These conditions can lead to Public Enemy #1: frustration.

1. **Pressure toward outcomes**. When staff feel pressured to get results that may not be within realistic time frames, their psychological need for control is not being met. The result is rising frustration and stress, which can lead to lower engagement and productivity.

2. **Punishment contingencies**. Engaged employees show up to work wanting to be able to perform their duties to the best of their abilities. The use of punishments and penalties can stifle any performance once again creating frustration, especially when some of the results are not within an employee's sole responsibility.

3. **Goal or strategy imposition**. Imposed goals without any input from employees can set unattainable targets, or perhaps targets

without sufficient meaning. This can lead to frustration and a lack of direction for the employees.

4. **Control types of rewards**. These are certain types of rewards or incentives that are tied directly to meeting certain performance goals. They tend to be the same for all individuals who meet those goals, lacking personalization and a practice of recognizing employees for their individual performance. If the goals are not met, there is no reward for anyone on the team. One of the results is increased frustration directed toward employees who may appear not to be carrying their share of the load.

5. **Performance evaluations**. In education and sports, for example, performance is an ongoing daily or weekly process. And the evaluations occur with the purpose of growing and improving performance, rather than looking for flaws. Chip and Dan Heath, in their bestselling book, *The Power of Moments*, say it is better to build peaks than it is to fix potholes.[3] Performance evaluations should focus on identifying, and building on, strengths. A great deal of them don't.

6. **Surveillance as a form of supervision.** Surveillance of any type has a direct impact on the trust in the relationship between supervisors and employees. When the need or desire for trust is not being met, frustration results.

When the psychological need for control is frustrated, it has a direct negative impact on an individual's internal motivation and thwarts their need for self-determination. When psychological needs are being frustrated, the signs and symptoms of physical and mental illness can appear.

Keep in mind what William McKnight, former CEO of 3M, said, "If you put a fence around people, you get sheep."

SO NOW WHAT?

1. Do your employees know where the company is going, and why?
2. Do they know how the company plans to get there?

3. Do your employees have the resources to do their job?
4. Are they empowered to make decisions on how to best do their job?

10

COMPETENCE—THE SECOND LEG

People feel competent when they meet optimal challenges. Optimal is key. The ability to do something that is trivially easy does not lead to perceived competence. The feeling of being effective occurs spontaneously only when one has worked toward accomplishment that is within their area of competence. When a challenge is well beyond someone's competence or natural talents, it can lead to what I referred to as Public Enemy #1 in Chapter 6: frustration.

All people are striving for mastery, for affirmation of their own competence. You don't have to be at the top of the class, the first to finish, or the best in any one thing. You only need to take on a meaningfully personal challenge and give it your best. Two of the most powerful motivators are having the opportunity to learn and build skills, and having the opportunity to do your very best work.

Campbell at Jack Ady's Cancer Centre was on target when he said that competency means having the skills to solve problems and meet challenges successfully. He pointed me to a bold heading in their *Living Our Values, Together* document: "We strive to be our best and give our best." There is an understanding that being able to use personal strengths and talents at work is a key component for developing competence and mastery at the Centre.

At Western Financial, they are doing something different about employee engagement. Osachoff says, like many organizations, there are numerous opportunities for internal or external formal training for our employees. However, there is a more direct focus on employee engagement at Western.

First and foremost, they have a specific Western Engagement Committee. Professional development and training in employee engagement is a core priority. As mentioned earlier, they survey to collect meaningful data across their organization. Lisa told me that "once a team has their team engagement score, we provide them with a significant amount of support. We give them the raw data, a focused PowerPoint presentation, a tool called *Employee Engagement: A Manager's Guide*, and a *Manager's Meeting Guide* with a link to an action plan. We provide additional support and tools for any teams with low engagement results."

Six months after the initial engagement survey, they "conduct a follow-up to review engagement with directors and above to see how each region is doing. This enables us to celebrate successes and support improvements much earlier across the organization."

As one of the legs on the three-legged stool, competence is critical to maintaining a balanced focus on purpose. There are five actions that leaders can take to enhance competence:

1. **Provide employees with optimal challenges in their work.** Problem-solving is a natural human skill. People like to rise to most of the challenges they encounter during their careers and lives. The Goldilocks Effect says the challenges shouldn't be so easy that they don't challenge the skills of the individual. Nor should they be too difficult or beyond the range of skills of the individual. The challenges should be optimal. They should be just right.

2. **Provide positive feedback.** One research paper's findings indicated that approximately 80 percent of managers said they provided feedback to their employees. However, the same study indicated that only about 20 percent of employees said they received feedback from their manager. What a tremendous disconnection. Feedback is critical for an individual to determine if they are on track in meeting or exceeding their roles and responsibilities.

3. **Personalize any rewards or incentives.** If you know some of your employees' personal history and interests, it is much more effective

to personalize the reward so that it relates to them personally. It shows you have taken the time to get to know and understand them. They are more than just a generic employee.

4. **Seize teachable moments**. The human brain is built with a need to learn. It is part of our desire to improve ourselves in the service of others. As a result, it is important to help employees expand their skills and competence. Teachable moments are extremely valuable, but must be approached with a sense of empathy and understanding of the individual's learning preferences.

5. **Ensure the best possible fit between the employee and their job**. Assigning tasks and delegating responsibilities is an art, not just a function of being a manager or supervisor. It can be particularly frustrating for any employee to be put into a role that doesn't match their natural strengths and talents.

It is easy to infer that not doing any of the five actions above will lead to low employee engagement, frustration, higher levels of stress, and the resulting physical or mental illness symptoms. Being aware of these five strategies will help you know where to focus your efforts in reducing any level of frustration of the need for competence.

We all have natural talents and strengths. When we have the opportunity to use them and share them with others, we create a sense of meaning and purpose in our lives. It creates feelings of positive stress. Not using our gifts and talents can bring distress. With distress comes our bodies' responses: a variety of physical and mental health illnesses. Not using our strengths and competencies can cause us to feel pent up, to feel a kind of cognitive push-pull in our minds and hearts. This being pulled back and forth in our minds can lead to poor performance and productivity.

The truism, "an investment in knowledge always pays the best interest," is attributed to Benjamin Franklin. As two legs of the three-legged stool, competence and control are complementary growth forces that lead people to become increasingly accomplished and maintain a healthy lifestyle. For all of the psychological needs, it is really the person's perceptions that matter. Their perceptions are their realities. People need to *feel* that they are effective and self-determining in their careers and personal lives. Other people's opinions should not make a difference to an individual.

SO NOW WHAT?

1. Are your employees using their best skills on the job on a regular basis?
2. Are they being given challenging work that stretches their abilities and knowledge?
3. Are they being given opportunities for additional training or learning?
4. What systems or parts of systems might be impeding employee efforts in the competence/mastery area?

11

CONNECTION—THE THIRD LEG

Employees need to feel connected with others while also feeling effective and in control. This is called the need for connection, and it leads people to be part of groups: families, social groups, work teams, sports teams, art clubs, etc. When people belong to a group, the group becomes part of their identity. They are naturally inclined to accept the group's values and ways of operating.

Herb Kelleher, cofounder of Southwest Airlines, said, "I feel that you have to be with your employees through all their difficulties, that you have to be interested in them personally. I want them to know that Southwest will always be there for them." That is a strong symbol of connection in any organization! In highly engaged companies, managers understand the power of engagement, so they design more interesting jobs and allow employees the opportunity to participate in decision-making.

Leaders can take eight actions to facilitate and enhance connections in the company:

1. **Create a compelling purpose**: one with which all employees can personally connect.
2. **Empathy**: take the time to understand employee concerns from their perspective.
3. **Warmth & inclusion**: all employees should have the opportunity to feel included and to feel the warmth of being an accepted part of the team or organization.

4. **Acknowledge emotions**: don't be afraid of acknowledging the emotions of employees who might be struggling at work.
5. **Convey respect for the individual**: identify the behaviours that support the value of respect; describe what behaviours are acceptable and which are not.
6. **Create feelings of value and significance**: simply taking the time to acknowledge someone's work gives them a sense of self-worth and significance in the organization.
7. **Care/concern when facing challenges**: most employees like, and prefer, to have some level of support when they are facing significant challenges at work.
8. **Opportunities to contribute and give**: individuals feel a greater degree of connection when they are given the opportunity to contribute to a project, a team, or the organization.

KB Heating has an innovative way to build on connection for their employees. Murakami says, "One of the things we do is to encourage employees to become involved in organizations in the community that are directly or indirectly related to our business. We have employees on the board of directors of the local construction association, chamber of commerce, and local apprenticeship committee. We encourage our employees to join committees of those organizations to offer their technical expertise." I noted that this is directly related to their purpose of being a community–involved organization.

When asked about the psychological need for connection at the Jack Ady Cancer Centre, Campbell was direct and to the point. "One of our core values is compassion. In our *Living Our Values, Together* document, this means that employees show kindness and empathy for all in our care, and for each other." I was excited to see compassion and empathy, two key components, as part of their everyday culture.

There was another core value that was clearly stated: diversity. The same document indicates that "we value diversity by being inclusive of all backgrounds, cultures, abilities, genders, perspectives, opinions, and approaches. We inspire trust by welcoming and equally valuing all in our care, those we serve, and those with whom we work." How can employees not connect with their patients and fellow workers working in a culture that focuses on, and supports, diversity!

At Western Financial, Osachoff works at creating a connection to the overall purpose of the company for all employees. "Having clear business goals and a clear purpose that identify how you contribute to the organizational success is the fundamental element of this. I think the hiring is crucial. You need to hire teams that represent diversity. That creates healthy balanced teams that have an enriched experience. People you hire need to understand your mission, vision, strategy, and culture. They have to want to be part of this. They need to fit in and align with it."

Notice again the focus on diversity. Also notice the emphasis on wanting to fit in and align with the company. Employees have a built-in need to feel like they belong, like they are part of something bigger than themselves, and that they are making a contribution in their world.

There are three conditions that can undermine connections and relationships at work. These can interfere with satisfying the need for connection and create varying degrees of frustration, which can have a negative impact on employee engagement.

1. **"Cold' or impersonal interactions**: you know the type—a half-hearted greeting in the morning, instructions that are given impersonally with little or no banter or discussion.
2. **Lack of engaged workplace**: most people want to be able to come to work engaged and to know that their co-workers are equally engaged and contributing to the overall goals.
3. **Negative work environment**: most employees will shrink away from a work environment that has negative aspects to it, like a complaining, blaming environment where it is always someone else's fault, or no one knows as much as the complaining individual(s).

"Take away my factories and I will build a new and better factory; but take away my people and grass will grow on the factory floor," Andrew Carnegie is quoted as saying. The most often overlooked but most important asset any organization has is its people. Feeling connected to the company, its purpose, other employees, and your customers is critical to maintaining good relationships and high employee engagement. You can't afford to overlook it!

I live in Alberta, located in an agricultural area just south of Calgary. Each spring, farmers plant their crops using a variety of seeds. Once each seed is planted, it will usually grow into a plant because it is the nature of seeds to do so. But not all seeds become plants that can be harvested later in the year. Some may shrivel and decompose and some may not sprout at all. Those that do may fail to thrive because the climate is inadequate or the necessary nutrients are lacking. They need sun, warmth, water, and the right temperatures. These elements do not *make* the plants grow; each plant is genetically encoded to grow. But they need the nutrients and environment that support and encourage their growth. This allows the plants to do what they do naturally.

In the same way, human beings need psychological nutrients to do what they do naturally. They must experience satisfaction in their four needs of purpose, control, competence, and connection. As the four parts of the three-legged stool, all are required for engagement and meaningfulness to occur.

We are biologically, cognitively, mentally, and physically wired to be connected to, and belong with, other human beings. The absence of belonging and connection is one of the leading causes of physical and mental illness. Frustration of the need for connection can cause you to experience anxiety, depression, loneliness, eating disorders, addiction, rage, blame, resentment, grief, or any of the many responses to stress your body uses. Are these the types of crops you want to harvest in your company?

It is up to business leaders to ensure that their employees are supported in the development of the four psychological needs. It is up to the organization to provide the purpose, the *why*, of what the employees are doing. It is purpose that binds the legs together, just as the legs support the seat of purpose.

Brené Brown, in *The Gifts of Imperfection*, said connection is "the energy that exists between people when they feel seen, heard, and valued; when they give and receive without judgement; when they derive sustenance and strength from their relationships."[1] The three-legged stool is about connection. Take the time to look after it—it can't look after itself.

Whew!! You have been exposed to some major concepts that actually form the very foundation of your organization. You may be feeling a bit overwhelmed at this point, wondering 'where do I start?', 'how do I implement this into my company.' Take heart! The following chapter, *Seven Simple Tools, One Simple Plan*, is your guide to developing your easy-to-use Employee Engagement Plan.

However, developing a plan and successfully executing that plan are two different things in the real world. *Execution – the Karate Way, Four Enemies of Execution*, and *The Window, The Mirror, and Engagement* are designed to help you successfully meet the challenge of execution head on–and survive!

SO NOW WHAT?

1. Are your employees functioning efficiently as a team? How do you know?
2. Does each employee feel a sense of belonging to their team or organization? How do you know?
3. Does your organization have a clear purpose statement that draws emotions and creates a strong sense of commitment to the team and the organization? How do you know?
4. Do you check in with your staff to see how they are *really* doing?

12

SEVEN SIMPLE TOOLS, ONE SIMPLE PLAN

Organizations today use a dizzying array of software dashboards that are information rich. Dashboards provide business leaders with quick looks into the operation of their organization. The software highlights the key points that need to be monitored throughout the year.

One of the most important dashboards is the financial dashboard, which provides information on key business ratios and trends. Another is the productivity dashboard, which monitors manufacturing outputs, delays, and targets.

The amount of information these types of dashboards provide is enormous and sometimes very complex. So many times we complicate our paths with too many options in what we are trying to monitor and achieve. This can quite often be overwhelming and lead to a high degree of procrastination and frustration.

Consider Ockham's Razor, a principle that was created in the fourteenth century by a Franciscan friar by the name of William of Ockham. The principle suggests that, all things being equal, you should prefer the simplest explanation for a phenomenon, or the simplest possible solution to a problem.

For my clients, I have created one of the simplest dashboards possible to start learning about purpose and employee engagement in their organizations. There are only seven tools to monitor on this dashboard. That's it—just seven. The tools are not designed to be prescriptive or restrictive in nature. They are designed to provide room for you to use your rational, emotional, and instinctive ways of thinking. They provide you with the flexibility to use each tool in ways that best suit your operational style.

So let's get started.

TOOL 1: THE MAGIC OF INDEX CARDS

The first tool on your dashboard involves using blank 3" x 5" index cards. From the janitor's room to the boardroom, give each person one blank card and ask them to answer one question: "Besides making a profit, why does this company do what it does?" If you're asked for clarification, I urge you not to answer. To get the results you are looking for, just let your employees write their answer to the question on their card based on their own interpretation.

Some employees may confuse this with trying to remember what the vision, mission, and values of the company are. They may even be looking for them on the wall to use for their answer. Let them, do not correct them. Remember, a purpose statement is the *why* of the organization, not the what, who, when, where, or how. Discovering this through this exercise is very valuable to employee engagement.

This brief activity will give you a wealth of information that will definitely surprise you. You will receive a wide variety of answers to show you how clear your company's purpose truly is (or, more likely, isn't) amongst all employees in the organization.

This information is worth its weight in index cards! Email works OK for this task but it's not as much fun as doing it in groups. The comments and discussions after the exercise are great and help increase overall connection and engagement.

To finish this task, review all of the cards. Observe and analyze the results you received. That's it—the first dashboard task is complete!

TOOL 2: SURVEY TO GO DEEP

Your second tool will help you identify the basic psychological needs of purpose, control, competence, and connection in your organization. It will do this through a series of questions that are directly related to the presence or absence of each need. This tool is a slightly more complex survey to gather information deeper in the organization.

To be sure, there are many metrics that can be used to measure different aspects of employee engagement that are not included in this book. For example, employee retention is one measurement of employee engagement and it is relatively easy to measure.

But it does not necessarily tell you *why* employees are staying or leaving. They could be staying because they are engaged with the overall purpose of the company, because many of their friends work there, because the job's not that bad, or because they feel trapped and might not feel they are employable somewhere else. Which type of employee do you want in your organization?

It is difficult to find any one survey tool that just focuses exclusively on the four key psychological needs of purpose, control, competence, and connection. These four needs underlie all other measures of employee engagement. If they're not satisfied, employee stress goes up, productivity drops, costs rise, and profitability goes down.

For my clients, I have created two different lengths of engagement surveys that are ideal for businesses of various sizes. Both focus exclusively on the four psychological needs.

The first one is called *Employee Engagement and Purpose Survey (Brief)*. It has twenty multiple-choice questions, and four open-ended questions. It takes six or seven minutes to complete. A free PDF version of this survey is available at www.rippledynamics.com. I encourage you to download this free resource to get started on your journey.

The second survey is called *Employee Engagement and Purpose Survey*. There are additional multiple choice and open–ended questions to collect additional information from each respondent. This longer version is available for purchase at www.rippledynamics.com.

There is one key aspect of any survey that is important to remember. Surveys primarily provide a snapshot of data based on how each respondent felt at the time of responding. It is important to take the time to share and discuss this data with your employees.

TOOL 3: GO DEEPER WITH DISCUSSION

Tool 3 is a frank and open discussion with your leaders, managers, and employees. The information you have collected allows you to probe deeper into the results to determine any underlying feelings, thoughts, or biases. It takes you below the basic answers and responses that you have collected so far using Tools 1 and 2.

It is time to start talking with your employees, customers, and shareholders. It is also time to get their input as to what is creating both the stronger and weaker aspects of the results you received. This is a key part of true employee engagement, giving your employees a sense of control and connection to their work and organization by listening to and discussing their input.

Discussions can help you identify and celebrate your organization's strengths. They also involve identifying ways to resolve the problems that are giving off warning signs on the dashboard.

The first process must be the development of a clear, concise purpose statement. You want one that is worthy of the WWII password challenge talked about earlier in Chapter 8.

A clear purpose statement provides your employees with an emotional connection to your company. Review the data from your survey and discussions that relate specifically to purpose. Chapter 8, *What's Your Purpose?*, is the starting point for creating your own purpose statement. Appendix A, *Sample Purpose Statements*, is also an integral part of this process.

From this, start to build your purpose statement, being sure to include employee input. Try to match one of the formats illustrated in Chapter 8 or Appendix A.

The next area to examine is the sections of the survey that relate to the three legs of control, competence, and connection. Find and review the survey questions that relate to each need along with the previous related chapters and questions. Collect the discussion information related to each need. Identify your strengths and define strategies to shore up any weaker areas in them.

TOOL 4: ONE-YEAR ACTION PLAN

The information that you collected in your dashboard surveys and from your discussions play another important role. It can act as a benchmark at the beginning of your annual program, giving you something to measure against at the end of the year. Based on your discussions with your employees, managers, and leaders, now is the time to set target scores, goals, and specific tasks for the coming year. You can use your preferred planning format for doing this.

By the way, this is not the time to use BHAGs (Big Hairy Audacious Goals). This is the time to set achievable, meaningful targets based on your information. If you have a few BHAGS in your current business plan, now is the time to see which ones effectively align with and support your core purpose. Perhaps they need to be revised.

It is also important that you set specific check-in points over the course of the year. Check-in points can provide opportunities to check the pulse of your organization.

TOOL 5: PULSE CHECKS

This tool is designed to help you maintain your course by monitoring strategic points throughout the year. At each of your check-in points, conduct a quick pulse check.

You can do this by using a brief format of your survey that focuses on the areas you are trying to improve. By brief, I mean from one to four questions that can be completed quickly and not take too much time out of an employee's work day. The pulse check should focus on one need at a time. For example, if purpose is one of your key targets for the year, select a few items from your survey that relate to purpose, send them out, and collect the results.

It is sometimes useful to use one or two of the related multiple-choice questions and one or two of the open-ended questions from your survey. Remember: you are just taking a pulse, quick and simple.

Compare the responses for these questions to the same questions in the original survey. Share your results with your employees. Make any revisions to your plan that may be indicated from your pulse check data.

Pulse checks are opportunities to see if you are heading in the desired direction. They provide you with opportunities to celebrate small successes along the way. They also prevent you from getting to the end of the year and finding out you were having problems.

TOOL 6: ONE-YEAR RESULTS

At the end of your first year, repeat the processes included in Tools 1 and 2 on your Employee Engagement Dashboard: the index card activity and full survey. Review the signs and symptoms of strengths and needs this new survey identified. Compare your results against the benchmarks you measured at the beginning of the year, then against the targets you set for the end of the year.

Share the results with your employees and get their input once again. Keep their engagement high by gathering and valuing their input.

TOOL 7: CELEBRATE & REPEAT THE CYCLE

First and foremost, celebrate your successes with your employees!

Second, circle back to Tool 3 and repeat the process for the coming year. You shouldn't need to create a new purpose statement if you created one at the beginning of the year. You may only want to modify it for additional clarity and simplicity, if necessary.

If you look back over the seven tools, you will see that most of the heavy lifting of the project is at the beginning of the year, especially in year one. As you continue each year, the process will become easier. Don't be overwhelmed by the processes outlined in this chapter. They really are that simple if prioritized and executed one at a time.

To help with the execution of your plan, I have included a section after Chapter 16 titled *How Can I Help You*. The following three chapters are focused directly on the keys and challenges to successful execution.

The word priority means "precedence in right or rank," or "the very first thing." There can only be one first thing, only one most important thing. Today, leaders have many priorities, several of them competing for the same organizational resources. But only one can be the very first thing, the most important thing. Don't let a list of multiple priorities confuse your thinking or decision making. Stay focused on one priority, *the* priority, and complete the task. Then put another task into the priority hot seat. And remember, each new priority task must be directly connected to enhancing employee engagement in your business or organization.

Raising employee engagement is not a race to the finish because there is no finish line. Market conditions change, employees retire, new employees join, and leadership can change. As you will see in the final chapter, purpose is a long game.

Vince Lombardi was born on June 11, 1913, and lived through two World Wars and the Great Depression. He is most known for coaching the Green Bay Packers football team to eight NFL Championships. Under his guidance, the Packers also won the first two Super Bowls in the 1966 and 1967 NFL seasons. Acknowledged by many as the greatest coach in NFL history, Lombardi left the world with many quotes and quips that have provided the backdrop to many business commentaries. Among them: "Winning is not a sometime thing; it's an all the time thing. You don't win once in a while. You don't do things right once in a while. You do them right all the time. Winning is a habit."

Being on purpose in your business has to become that winning habit.

SO NOW WHAT?

1. Take action right now. Implement Tool 1, the index card exercise, as soon as possible!

13

EXECUTION—THE KARATE WAY

I have trained in Fudokan-Shotokan karate for thirty-eight years as both a student and instructor. I have been fortunate to achieve my fifth-degree black belt during that time and I continue my training on a weekly basis. My instructor, Sensei (teacher) Zorislav Krco (pronounced 'kerso'), a seventh-degree black belt, immigrated to Alberta from Serbia as the wars in the former Yugoslavia were going on. He lives about two hours away and I commute once a week to continue my training.

I have also been fortunate to train each year with Sensei Krco's instructor, seventy-eight-year old, ninth-degree black belt Sensei Vladimir Jorga (pronounced Yorga). Sensei Jorga resides in Belgrade, Yugoslavia, and travels around the world teaching students in his organization, the International Traditional Fudokan Karate Federation.

Sensei Yorga travels to Alberta at least once per year to train the students at Sensei Krco's club. A great deal of the training when he visits is very physically demanding, requiring strength, stamina, speed, and flexibility. Senior students (brown and black belts) are pushed to their limits time and time again over the three days.

However, there is a psychological and philosophical side of karate that Sensei Jorga imparts to his senior students as a result of his sixty-plus years of training. But he imparts it through the physical training itself. Five important principles related to the execution of technique have been drilled into our minds for the past several years, over and over again, so that they become natural.

Like the martial arts, leading a business is a deeply personal endeavour. In karate, we are taught to adapt our techniques to the uniqueness of our bodies; the philosophy of karate recognizes that no two bodies are exactly alike. I have trained with, and taught, students of all ages and different body types who have successfully continued their training through to their black belts.

Similarly, leaders approach their roles in ways that are specific to their personality and temperament, skills and training, communication styles, and past experiences. Regardless of what courses they have taken, books they have read, or seminars they have attended, each leader comes away with their own perspective. It is this unique perspective that results in the behaviours that their employees see. Employees zero in on these actions and behaviours for their own interpretation of the organization's culture.

PRINCIPLE 1

The first principle in the Karate Way is *gan* (look). Looking is required to create an awareness of the current situation in your organization. Looking involves doing a quick sweep of your business indicators. Traditionally, this means financial data related to profit and loss, and balance sheets. It can also include a review of employee performance indicators. These more traditional metrics only show the results of what has been going on at the surface of the business operations. They are indicators of what has happened in the past.

Looking also involves taking the indicators and making a deeper examination of the behaviours and processes that created these results. You are looking for strengths to leverage and challenges to resolve. Looking is about creating a deeper awareness of your business. You are looking in order to clearly identify your purpose, your prime target. It is about looking to develop an awareness of the situation around you, within the culture of your organization. Awareness needs to focus on the strengths, challenges, roles, and responsibilities in your organization.

Awareness, or looking, should precede all actions at all stages of planning and execution. Only with awareness can we completely understand the strengths and challenges in our organization and in our personal lives. The most important thing that you should always be looking at or being aware of, is your purpose. Remember, purpose trumps everything. So, first, look.

PRINCIPLE 2

Principle two is *soku* (orient). In karate, this means orienting your feet and body toward your opponent. In business, it is important to orient your business in the direction in which your purpose is pulling you. Your purpose should be powerful and emotional enough to actually pull you into your future.

Let's consider this concept by using a common, everyday rubber band. If you have time, it works best if you actually go get one—make sure it's not too thick! Now, hold the rubber band lightly between your two thumbs without stretching it. Your left thumb represents where you are today and your right thumb represents where you would like to go. If you move your right thumb away from your left one while holding your left thumb steady, the rubber band begins to stretch and resist. In a simplistic sort of way, this is how our minds are programmed. Something is changing, and we initially want to take the pressure off by returning back to the way things are. This is perfectly normal!

Now, stretch the rubber band between your thumbs to its fullest extension, without breaking it—you can feel the increasing pressure in the band to return to normal, to stop stretching. Our lives are like that. Every time we stretch ourselves or our businesses, we grow and learn new things. Sometimes, this is not enough to break free from doing things the way they've always been done. Change is hard. We must be looking at the change we want to implement and we must orient our employees and resources toward where we are looking. Hang onto that rubber band—you will need it again later in the chapter.

PRINCIPLE 3

The third principle in karate is *tan* (focus). When training or fighting, we must focus our techniques using the power of our hips to increase the power of our hands and feet. Similarly, all an organization's resources and all the stakeholders must be focused on the same clear purpose.

Alexa Hirschfeld, CEO of the Paperless Post, said that, in her business, "the biggest challenge is to stay focused. It's to have the discipline when there are so many competing things." Purpose trumps everything but, by itself, it's not enough. It is only the seat of the three-legged stool. There needs to be an equal focus on the three legs: control, competence, and connection. Balance and focus on the future can only occur when all four parts of the stools are in sync with each other. Support needs to be provided for all individuals for the development and encouragement of their needs for control, competence, and connection.

PRINCIPLE 4

Principle four is *ryoku* (execute). In karate, once we have our eyes on the target and our feet properly oriented in our chosen stance, and have started to relax our body and focus on the power in our abdomen and hips, we need to actually *execute* the technique.

Herein lies one of the major problems for many organizations. At the organization level, a new or revised strategic plan can be created annually with goals, strategies, and responsibilities clearly laid out. At the personal level, many people set out New Year's resolutions or annual goals of different types. Effective and successful execution is the primary stumbling block for both organizations and individuals, which leads us to the final principle.

PRINCIPLE 5

The fifth principle is *hashin* (commit whole body and mind). When executing a technique of any kind, whether it is punching, striking, kicking, or blocking, we had to learn to fully commit to our technique, not only with our body but with our mind as well. It is the mind that holds the power to focus all of the body, starting with initiating the technique and ending with the proper execution of the technique.

Think of yourself as the leader, the mind of the organization and think of your organization as the body, all of the other working components. Grab that rubber band again and stretch it between your thumbs like before. Now I want you to actually experience the concept of *hashin*.

Once again, hold your left thumb stationary to represent where you are at right now. Use your right thumb to pull and stretch the rubber band. You will again feel that elastic pressure building, trying to pull the right thumb back toward the left.

By now, you should have the rubber band stretched to its maximum limit without breaking. At least two uncertainties exist: first, how long you can hold the rubber band at maximum stretch before your arms start to shake and you begin to tire; second, how far you can go before the band breaks, causing one of your thumbs to feel some pain from the snapback of the broken band.

OK, let's remove the uncertainty. Stretch the rubber band until it breaks. Keep going! Come on, make it break! Did it hurt?

You have now experienced a small version of *hashin*. You knew from previous experience that breaking a rubber band can have painful consequences. As hard as you tried to stretch the band past the breaking point, your mind wasn't fully focused on completing the technique because of that anticipation. Once you actually broke the band, you had completely executed your technique. And . . . you did it in spite of any anticipated consequences. Congratulations!

The first time I did this with a group of financial advisors, I gave each person a choice of rubber bands of different thicknesses and lengths. Some chose thinner ones, some chose the thicker ones. Ever watch a group of grown men and women slowly stretching rubber bands until they break? It doesn't look pretty! Looks of apprehension, heads turned to one side, an eye or two closed, a grimace of anticipation of the impending pain. Ever listen to a bunch of people who've had rubber bands break on them? Sorry, I can't repeat some of the comments here.

There is another side to the analogy of the rubber band. You were experiencing a type of procrastination as you tried to keep the rubber band fully stretched. You also experienced the potential use of a lot of energy trying to slowly break the rubber band. There's another way to break the rubber band—if you're up to it, grab a new one and use the same technique. This time, though, break it quickly.

When you do, you will probably not notice a significant difference in how much pain you felt. But you used up a lot of energy doing it the slow way because you were always fighting the pull. In life, we sometimes think that procrastinating saves energy because it seems easier than tackling a project or task. However, as you can see and feel, the energy used over long periods of continual procrastination is much greater than the energy to simply complete an action or task.

Hashin is a critical part of execution for companies and organizations of all types. Many times, changes get talked about, employee engagement gets discussed around the management table, new initiatives get strategized but, in the end, little takes place. Masayoshi Son, CEO of Softbank and Softbank Mobile, says, "Think big; think disruptive. Execute with full passion." That is *hashin*.

As you will see in the next chapter, many times the enemies of execution get in the way. Your execution must follow the five principles: first, look; second, orient; third, focus; fourth, execute; fifth, commit your entire body and mind.

Absolute commitment at all levels of the organization is necessary in order for execution to be as successful as possible. It is also required to achieve the company's purpose. Perhaps author Sue Grafton said it best: "Ideas are easy. It's the execution of ideas that really separates the sheep from the goats."

SO NOW WHAT?

1. What is the most effective way of looking at your business?
2. How will you identify the strengths, challenges, and gaps in your organization?
3. Are you focused on your organization's purpose? Are your actions and behaviours aligned with your purpose?

4. What will it take to fully execute your plan with your whole body and mind focused on your true purpose?

14

THE FOUR ENEMIES
OF EXECUTION

The fourth and fifth steps of the Karate Way, execution and total commitment, are where many organizations come up short. Phrases like "paralysis by analysis" and "destination procrastination" quickly come to mind. But there is a lot more going on related to these phrases that helps us understand them. Let's look a bit deeper.

There are four enemies of execution that affect all business leaders at some point in their career. The four enemies are surprise, fear, doubt, and indecision, and they operate at the psychological and emotional levels of our brains. They can be very difficult to recognize but, once you do, your awareness of them takes away most of their power. Notice that I said 'most of' and not 'all.' Because these enemies operate at the emotional level, they have a great deal of power over our rational thinking.

SURPRISE

Surprise refers to anything that causes some level of astonishment or shock. It is a feeling caused by something unexpectedly happening.

In business, surprises can happen in many ways. Consider a significant parts price increase from a large supplier. Your business operating expenses may not be able to withstand the impact. It is always important for business leaders to be aware of as many factors in their environment as possible. Remember the first principle of execution: look. However, it is still possible for factors to arise unexpectedly and create a surprise or challenge to deal with.

FEAR

Fear is a distressing emotion aroused by impending danger, evil, pain, or any potential negative event. Fear is an apprehensive or uneasy feeling, whether the threat is real or imagined.

Fear can be experienced in different ways. One of the most overriding fears that affects many businesses is a fear called the scarcity mentality. "There won't be enough business." "We can't afford to buy parts." "What if my best employee leaves?" "What if a new competitor opens up?" "What if my cash flow is not high enough this month?"

The scarcity mentality is one way of viewing the world on a rating scale, with scarcity at one end and abundance at the other. Scarcity is characterized by a perception of apparently limited resources that are insufficient to meet the needs of all businesses. There is only a finite amount of resources and wealth in the world. When one person gets some, another person loses some. It is sometimes called the zero-sum paradigm of life. From a business perspective, more is better. Scarcity is characterized by competitively comparing your business to others. There is a competition for both resources and wealth.

On the other hand, abundance is about situations where there are more than enough resources for everyone. Collaboration, not competition, creates prosperity and what you appreciate gains value. From this perspective, wealth is being created all the time by people who are highly motivated. Whenever a person acquires something, it causes more wealth for others. Abundance is characterized, not by competition, but by cooperation and sharing. In recognizing that there are enough resources and business for everyone, you can take away the fear of scarcity, that you will be losing out on something.

You can rate yourself on the *Scarcity vs. Abundance Mentality Scale*. Download your free PDF copy at www.rippledynamics.com. See where you fall on the continuum between scarcity and abundance thinking. I think the results will surprise you!

DOUBT

Fear is closely related to the third enemy of execution: doubt. Doubt is fear turned inward. It is a lack of confidence in one's skills in any situation. Doubt is a feeling of uncertainty or lack of conviction. It can be defined as believing something may not be true or is unlikely.

The enemies of surprise and doubt can cause you to get sidetracked by something other than the task at hand. It can be difficult to not get distracted by email, phone calls, people stopping in your office, etc. Many times, these types of distractions can pop out of nowhere. But they need to be acted on as soon as possible.

These distractions can also occur because of self-doubt in your ability to tackle the large project or be ready for the presentation. This is a form of procrastination that results from making the short-term decision to do something that is perhaps less onerous or more interesting than the important project at hand.

INDECISION

The three first fears all lead to the deadliest enemy of execution in organizations: indecision. Indecision is a feeling of wavering between two or more courses of action. Sometimes indecision is referred to as hesitation, which is not accurate. Hesitation is the direct result of feeling indecisive. Hesitation is one of the behaviours that results from the emotion of feeling indecisive.

Indecision acts as handcuffs for many organizations and confuses employees. This is where "walking the talk" starts to break down. It is something that seasoned employees have been through many times and they may be suspect of any effort to change. Indecision over longer periods of time is called procrastination, a disease of certainty in stifling creativity, employee engagement, and productivity.

Indecision can lead to failing to get started on a particular project, action, or strategy. Failure getting started can show up in three forms.

The **first** is not remembering to act. This can result from postponing acting until a suitable opportunity presents itself. This, in turn, can lead to letting good opportunities slip by while waiting to catch a bigger one you think is coming. Not remembering to act can also result from dealing with too many things at once—spinning too many plates on sticks, so to speak. When your mind is over-tasked, it loses some of its ability to filter in the information it needs. This means that some good opportunities are filtered out of all of the incoming data and missed altogether.

Indecision also leads to a **second** factor, which is not recognizing that a good time to get started has arrived. This gets more acute when deadlines are involved. The best time to start an initiative may have arrived but is not recognized as such by the person in charge.

The **third** factor in failing to get started is an initial reluctance to act now vs. acting later. Your desired behaviour might be a trade-off between waiting patiently for long-term results or experiencing short-term rewards now. Many times, it's easier to make the short-term trade off because of the more immediate rewards. We avoid planning too far out in the future by responding to the apparent rewards of today.

All four enemies of execution – surprise, fear, doubt, and indecision – can result in a lot of unfinished tasks piling up. Overextending yourself by pursuing multiple tasks is like being a spinner of multiple plates on multiple sticks. Each time you take on a new task, have an interruption to deal with, or an email or voice mail to respond to, you are spinning one more new plate on a new stick. Each plate represents an incomplete task, from work or your personal life. Every one of those plates is spinning in either your conscious or subconscious mind.

They are all there, slowly going from spinning to wobbling to teetering or falling off the stick. Each spinning plate requires an ongoing source of energy from your mind. All these plates have a significant impact on your level of stress, usually taking you from a position of positive stress (the stress we need to operate and be successful) to a position of negative stress—distress.

There are three ways to successfully deal with the spinning plates.

The **first** is to delegate as many plates as you can to those with the skills, interests, and time to complete them for you.

The **second** is to focus on one plate (task), complete it, and take it down.

The **third** is to recognize that perhaps a few of those wobbly plates don't need to be spun anymore. Simply take them down and get rid of them. Don't leave them in a desk or on a to-do list because they will still be spinning in your subconscious. Be ruthless and disruptive—stop doing whatever is not absolutely essential to the goals and purpose of your work.

If the stress of being over-loaded becomes too much, the next step will most likely be shutting down. You may look at the papers on your desk, scroll up and down your email list, or search the Internet for news or jokes. It may get to the point where you just spin your chair around and look out the window, where you stop performing and have a blank look on your face. Definitely a time for change!

What makes these four enemies so powerful? They are all feelings, they are based on emotions. Emotions are much more powerful than the rational, thinking part of our brain. Emotions can provide very challenging roadblocks to progress as shown above or they can be harnessed to provide significant horsepower for achieving your purpose.

Beneath the enemies of execution—beneath surprise, fear, doubt, and indecision—lurks Public Enemy #1: frustration. At this point, you are most likely feeling like you are off-purpose. You may also feel like you have no control or autonomy in your life because the job has temporarily taken over your ability to make effective choices. There may be moments when you doubt your skills or competency. Part of frustration is pulling away to some degree from others, feeling isolated from your team or organization. But all is not lost. Frustration of your psychological needs is only a temporary reaction to the situation that you are in. If you can change parts of your situation, you can change your behaviours.

One final point: It does not matter if you are actually physically over-loaded. Just *feeling* overloaded will cause your performance to drop and mistakes to go up.

Remember the four enemies of execution: surprise, fear, doubt, and indecision, and how they can lead to different degrees of frustration. The ancient Chinese military strategist Sun Tzu, wrote in *The Art of War*: "If you know the enemy and know yourself, you need not fear the results of a hundred battles." Like a good business leader, maintain an awareness of these four fears. As long as you do, you take away their power and you can definitely keep public enemy #1 at bay.

SO NOW WHAT?

1. Download and complete the free *Scarcity vs. Abundance Mentality Scale* at www.rippledynamics.com.
2. How does the scarcity mentality impact on you and your business?
3. What is one thing that you can start doing right away to shift your perception toward the abundance mentality?
4. Which of the enemies of execution are acting as barriers or challenges to being on purpose in your business or personal life?
5. Do you keep some type of to-do list? How many things on your current list relate directly to the purpose statement of your company?

15

THE WINDOW, THE MIRROR, AND ENGAGEMENT

Marcus Buckingham, in *Now, Discover Your Strengths*, describes our patterns of thinking and behaving as "our sense, our recurring pattern of thought, feeling or behaviour that is caused by our unique mental networks in our brain. These networks serve as filters, sorting and sifting the world we encounter, causing us to zero in on some stimuli and miss others entirely."[1] Our personal perceptions can be very difficult to identify and understand by ourselves.

In my experience, there are five characteristics related to filters and patterns of thought and perception that I find useful.

First, perceptions are common. Everyone on earth has their own way of looking at, and interacting with, their world. Every business or organization has a pattern of operating and behaving based on the people leading them.

Second, our patterns of thought are functional. They help us determine the boundaries of our lives and set the rules for success for operating within those boundaries. They help us determine which incoming information is important and which is not.

Third, sometimes our patterns of thought become the *only* patterns of thoughts or ways of doing things. This is sometimes called perception paralysis. It can be more commonly referred to as stubbornness. We become inflexible and think *our* way is the *only* way.

Fourth, our patterns of thought and ways of doing things need to be flexible during times of transition. It is important that we try to see things through the eyes of others.

Fifth, and, for me, the most important characteristic, is that we can all choose to change our perceptions or the way we see and interact with the world around us.

Viktor Frankl was a survivor of the Holocaust and the Nazi death camps. He was a psychiatrist when he was captured and put into a concentration camp. After his release, he rebuilt his practice and wrote *Man's Search for Meaning*. The following quote lends much credence to the fact that we can change our ways of thinking and behaving, if only we have the will or the purpose: "Everything can be taken from a man but one thing: the last of the human freedoms—to choose one's attitude in any given set of circumstances, to choose one's own way."

Being able to change our perceptions, our points of view, is a critical skill for business leaders. Think of standing in front of a window that looks out over the area where your employees are working. Just to the side of the window is a mirror that is about the same size as the window. The window and mirror are among the simplest yet most effective management and communication tools.

In his book, *Good to Great*, Jim Collins uses the metaphor of the window and the mirror to explain one of the characteristics of high-performing leaders. He says that these leaders use the window and mirror in a specific way to manage their companies. It is one of the key characteristics that sets them apart from low-performing leaders.

When things are going great in the business—when a project finishes on time, productivity is up, and shareholders are happy—these leaders look through the window out onto the shop floors or down the halls of the large office. They pass the recognition and praise on to their employees knowing they're essential components of success. By doing so, they are enhancing all of the components of the three-legged stool. They are highlighting competence and connection in their employees. They are helping the employees feel that they have had some control of the process along the way to success. They can see the rewards of their work as their organization works to achieve its purpose.

When things may not have gone so well—perhaps the project went into overtime, or there were some errors in production—these same high-performing leaders look in the mirror and take the responsibility for those things that went wrong. Even though they know that the work is being done by their team, they know that the performance and engagement of their teams starts with them.

What do the low-performing leaders do? It's a pretty simple answer actually. When things are not going so well, their first preference is to look through the window and blame the employees, blame the vendors, blame the market conditions. The responsibility and blame will fall anywhere but with them.

And if things are going great? Well, the first place they look is for their reflection in the mirror. If the goals were achieved, the profit margins were met, and the shareholders are happy, it is because they did it as leaders.

Low-performing leaders are impacted by a particular thinking or cognitive bias. It is called the *self-serving bias*. This describes the human tendency to blame external forces when bad things happen and to give ourselves credit when good things happen.

Think back to the window and the mirror. People who are generally unaware of the self-serving bias in themselves will look through the window to blame others or external circumstances. They will also look in the mirror when good things are happening in their company or on their team.

The self-serving bias is just one of many types of biases or errors that occur in our thinking. All humans are affected by these biases, some more so than others. Your biggest defense is *awareness* of your own thinking patterns and errors. Once you are aware of a thinking error like the self-serving bias, you can change your thinking pattern. You can then slowly change that new way of thinking into a new habit.

Let me put both types of leaders on a sliding scale. On one end there are the leaders that I like to call the "builders." At the other end are the "blamers," the ones who pass the buck when things go wrong. As with any scale, there are many degrees of difference in between as you slide a marker from one end of the scale to the other.

You, and only you, have the power and the control to place that marker on the scale where you feel you will be most effective in building employee engagement, improving productivity, and increasing profitability. You have control over how you use your window and mirror. You can control whether you choose to look into the mirror or out through the window, and, you can control how you react to what you see.

If you use your window and mirror with the right perspectives, you can build relationships, culture, and trust. You can make sure that you place some of the focus of control in the hands of your employees and provide them with the correct amount of resources. You can make sure that they feel competent in their jobs and provide them with avenues for new learning and experiences. You can help build and maintain positive, respectful connections throughout the company.

The window and the mirror are excellent tools for utilizing the power of the three-legged stool. Most importantly, you can convey the deep sense of purpose that guides your company and creates an environment of high employee engagement. Take a minute to think about how you would use, or perhaps are using, your window and mirror to support high employee engagement in your company. It's all about perception and how you decide to use each side.

It is good to keep in mind the saying of Lao Tzu, a sixth-century BC Chinese philosopher: "If you fail to honor your people, they will fail to honor you. It is said of a good leader that when the work is done, the aim fulfilled, the people will say, 'We did this ourselves.'"

SO NOW WHAT?

1. Are you a blame leader, a builder leader or somewhere in between?
2. How can you use your window and mirror to ensure that the company purpose is clearly understood and adopted throughout the organization?
3. How can you use your window and mirror to focus on meeting or enhancing the core psychological needs of control, competence, and connection in your business?

16

PURPOSE IS A LONG GAME

Employee engagement is not a one-shot wonder to raise engagement and then let it drift along at the side of the company, generally unnoticed and unattended to. Engagement is tied to self-motivation, which I have represented as the four parts of a three-legged stool. The three legs represent the three psychological needs of control, competence, and connection that support the seat. But it is the psychological need for purpose, the seat, that ties the three legs together.

Once a purpose for the organization has been identified and communicated, it becomes an organization's driving force, the emotional pull that keeps everyone focused on a future of making a difference in the lives of others. Purpose is a long game, and so is employee engagement. High employee engagement is a way of doing things; of creating job descriptions; of developing processes and procedures; of operations, and of customer relationships. A well-balanced three-legged stool leads to high engagement, improved productivity, and increased profitability.

I would like to introduce you to John Davidson, a man who exemplifies the understanding that purpose is a long game, that it is a way of both *being* and *doing*.

A splendid thing happened to John and Sherene Davidson on April 10, 1980. Their son, Jesse, came into their lives. Little did they realize the impact their child would have on them and thousands of others around the world. Raised in London, Ontario, with his older brother, Tyler, and younger brother, Tim, Jesse was diagnosed in 1986 with Duchenne Muscular Dystrophy (DMD), a life-threatening condition that affects boys, almost exclusively. Most of these boys have difficulty surviving beyond their mid-twenties.

John Davidson is a man with a purpose, a very well-defined purpose. He is also an avid walker. He went out for a long-distance walk not once but twice, and each time the walk changed his life, and the lives of his family and thousands of people who have been impacted by DMD. My brother, Hal, and I were fortunate enough to interview John for our first book, *Lifeworth, Finding Fulfillment Beyond Networth* in 2011. Here's some of the background from what came to be known as "Jesse's Journey."

In 1995, Jesse's father, John, who was forty-nine at the time, pushed Jesse in his wheelchair 3,300 kilometres across Ontario, from the Manitoba border to the Quebec border. The journey took 124 days on the road. It raised awareness of DMD and raised $1.5 million for research.

Three years later, on Jesse's eighteenth birthday, April 10, 1998, John dipped the toes of his running shoes in the Atlantic Ocean at Quidi Vidi, Newfoundland, just outside of St. John's. Two hundred and eighty-six days and 8,300 kilometres later, John dipped those same shoes in the Pacific Ocean, at Beacon Hill Park in Victoria, British Columbia. He and his support team had set a Guinness Book of Records for the fastest crossing of Canada on foot. The Jesse's Journey team had raised another $2 million for research and launched the Jesse Davidson Endowment, which has now reached almost $15 million.

Jesse Davidson, who passed away in 2009, left a significant legacy for the world. Jesse's shortened life was packed with adventures geared to raising both funds and awareness of DMD. During his short life, Jesse was honoured to join the 48th Highlanders Pipe and Drum Corp on the ice as he dropped the ceremonial puck on the opening night of the hockey season in Maple Leaf Gardens in Toronto. He met with former Prime Minister Jean Chrétien, and was given a standing ovation in the House of Commons. In 1996, Jesse received the Order of Ontario and, the following year, he was joined by Queen Elizabeth II in a tree-planting ceremony in London, Ontario. In 1998, Jesse flew to Paris to assist the French Muscular Dystrophy Association with its thirty-hour telethon. The telethon generated $116 million CDN.

In 2001, John Davidson released his first book, *Jesse's Journey: A Canadian Story*.[1] John's second book, *The Right Road: How Far Will You Go*,[2] was published in 2010. Both books are excellent reads with great stories surrounding the details, hardships, challenges, and successes of *Jesse's Journey*.

John said during our interview for *Lifeworth*, "Losing Jesse was the most difficult thing I have ever faced. Speaking to people about what is possible in life, about what Jesse managed to accomplish, and the legacy he left, helps me keep my son alive in my heart."

The twentieth anniversary of the walk across Canada occurred in 2018. To mark the year, John used his original journal notes to craft a weekly look back at the cross-Canada journey with pictures and reminiscences spanning the same time period of 286 days on the road. (The entire collection of weekly stories is available on John's blog at www.ordinaryhero.live.) It was through those newsletters that I learned how much has happened over the past twenty years. I reached out to John to discuss his perspective on how *Jesse's Journey* and his non-profit organization are helping people affected by Duchenne to find their sense of purpose, control, and competence in understanding DMD, and their need for connection to others. I also asked John how driving *Jesse's Journey* forward and to see it grow continued to meet his needs.

John is now a professional speaker (www.ordinaryhero.live) who continues to raise money in support of research in Jesse's name. "Every time I finish speaking, I take comfort in knowing that another group of people know what *Jesse's Journey* is all about," he told me. "Our story and my presentation are designed to speak to people in the audience about that thing inside them that they really want to do. I think a story about a father and son and their quest is something the audience can relate to. I give them a story and I want them to be inspired about their lives and their own world. I want them to think, *Hey, you know what? If things aren't right in my world, it's up to me to change things. And now I know that I can do that. I don't want a life of complaining about the way things are. I want to go out and do something about it.*"

By taking control of part of his life and Jesse's, John gave himself the opportunity to develop the competence and skillsets he and Jesse needed to guide them during the journey across Canada.

"The first morning when we started out in Ontario, we had no actual road history to fall back on. We were really in uncharted waters and were pretty much just making it up and learning with every new step. The important thing is you have to take that first step. It's that leap of faith into the unknown. You learn very quickly that you can't steal second base if you've still got a foot on first! By the time we reached Thunder Bay, we had developed a very solid routine and were working from a pattern. But you can't develop that pattern if you don't take those first steps. And even at that, I had no idea about the future and how things would grow and become what they are today."

There were no processes or systems for John and Jesse to follow. There was no endowment fund. They just started from the most basic of ideas and followed a dream, a goal, to create a larger awareness of Duchenne Muscular Dystrophy. What they did have was a deeper purpose that was driving both of them.

"When Jesse and I entered into this, we took this on very soberly, looking at the big picture. Lots of people do things when their child is alive and do their best at it. And then, when they have lost that child, that part of their life changes. I can understand their wanting to close that chapter on their lives and move on. These people have been to hell and back. What Jesse and I did was make a decision that we weren't doing what we were doing just for one boy. We were in it for all of the boys with DMD and that is still true today.

"Having said that, we would be the first to admit that we were pretty much amateurs at the beginning. But, then again, aren't we all really amateurs at the beginning, whether it's riding a bicycle, learning to skate, or kissing a girl? But for some reason, our story captured people's imagination and emotions. I think a lot of people asked themselves, *What would I do if that was me?*"

It was obvious that it was their common purpose that drove John and Jesse forward. It gave them the incentive to develop the competence and skills they needed as each new challenge or opportunity arose.

In a more contemplative part of our discussion, John said, "If I had to live my life over again, just like a stool, I would pick up the three things that matter the most to me and forget the rest."

In the conversation about replaying part of his life, John talked about how complex life is today and how swamped people are today.

"Their time is often being chewed up by the very technology that was designed to make life easier—their computers. We have reached the point where we are asking ourselves, *Is the computer working for me or am I working for the computer?* I have been unplugging from a lot of things and just retaining the ones that are really meaningful to me. My life now consists of speaking, gardening, and reviving my love of drawing. I say to people, 'Just enjoy who you really are. Nobody is more capable of being in control of your life than you are.'"

John and I spent some time talking about all of the changes in technology. We talked about social media, and the amount of negative content there. We talked about the speed of change, and the complete inundation of our lives by information, a great deal of which is meaningless to us.

Looking back on his days in broadcasting, John recalled a time when they had just twelve channels on their television and had to walk over to the TV to change the channel. He compared that to today's average household and its more than 100 channels.

"The big difference is that, twelve channels or 100 channels, we still have only one receiver: our brain. And when you bombard that brain time and time again with the disasters of the world as you channel surf, it's stressful. You begin to think that what you're seeing is an accurate reflection of the world and that it's hopeless for you to change anything. You couldn't be farther from the truth.

"We may have 100 or 500 channels, but since we have just one receiver, be particular about what you let in."

Then John issued a challenge: "When was the last time you stepped outside at night just to look up at the sky and the stars? When was the last time you actually stopped to smell the flowers?"

"We just don't take time to get to know who we are and get comfortable with who we are. We are so busy trying to live the lives we see on TV or in the media, or the lives of others around us who we foolishly think are living the 'perfect life.' Trust me, they're not."

John continued, "Are you living the life that is really you? Are you letting that life out or are you too busy letting everybody else's life in?"

Talking about his 286-day record-setting walk across Canada and the twenty years that have slipped by since then, John said, "My life's journey has really caused me to take a hard look at myself and to ask: What am I here for? We're just a tiny little fleck in the universe and we aren't here very long. When you get to the end, there has to be something meaningful. You want to be able to say with your last breath, 'I made a difference.' If you want to make a difference, you have to define *how* you want to make that difference.

"The whole Jesse Journey experience opened my eyes to how much you can do to help other people. There are millions of opportunities and too many of them go unanswered. It was a terrible, terrible thing that took me to the road in the first place. It was a wonderful, wonderful thing that came out of it."

There was a slight pause in the conversation and then John continued. "For the rest of my life, I hope to continue what I'm doing now, trying to be an inspiration and making a difference in the lives of others so that they can make a difference in somebody else's life."

John Davidson exemplifies the fact that being on purpose is a long game. That's the promise he made to his son. That's the promise he continues to keep every day!

Jim Rohn, entrepreneur, author, and motivational speaker, wrote, "Whatever good things we build end up building us." A business or an organization is a gift. It is an opportunity for business leaders, employees, shareholders, customers, and the public to make differences in the lives of others.

As a business leader, you can provide others with an opportunity that they may not ordinarily have. It is an opportunity for them to give to others through your company and for them to feel the connection and meaningfulness of making those gifts.

There's a popular Chinese proverb that says: "The best time to plant a tree was twenty years ago. The second best time is now." There is a wonderful challenge in that statement. Are you ready?

HOW CAN I HELP YOU?

I have created 6 ways for you to learn more about human behaviour, to access some of the resources that I have created, to provide you access to connecting with me, and to order additional books for your employees.

1. For help creating and implementing your employee engagement plan, developing your purpose statement, or for mentoring services through Ripple Dynamics Inc., contact me directly at the number and email below.

2. To access different types of resources, go to www.RippleDynamics. com
   - *Calculating The Potential Costs of Low Employee Engagement* (PDF)
   - *Scarcity vs. Abundance Mentality Scale* (PDF)
   - *Employee Engagement and Purpose Survey (Brief) (PDF)*
   - *Employee Engagement and Purpose Survey (available to purchase)*

3. For author interviews or speaking engagements, you can contact me at:
   > P: 403-394-9863
   > E: dana@rippledynamics.com

4. To learn more about human behaviour and dynamics in all areas, subscribe to the free newsletter, *Free Reining*, at www. RippleDynamics.com.

5. To inquire about discounts for ten or more copies of this book for individuals, corporations, organizations, or associations, contact me at the number and email above.

APPENDIX A
SAMPLE PURPOSE STATEMENTS

1. **GoldieBlox (girls' construction toys, books, games):** To correct the gender imbalance in engineering.
2. **Ministry of Supply (office wear retailer):** Clothing should be an extension of your body, equipping you to realize your limitless potential.
3. **Kurgo (pet accessories retailer):** To help people get out & safely enjoy the world with their dogs.
4. **Coca-Cola:** To refresh the world in mind, body, and spirit. To inspire moments of optimism and happiness through our brands and actions
5. **POC Medical Systems:** To develop next-generation diagnostics to provide a better life.
6. **Campbell Soup:** To serve as a leader, live a balanced life and apply ethical principles to make a significant difference.
7. **Kiva (microfinance company):** To connect people through lending to alleviate poverty.
8. **Life is Good (online retailer):** To spread the power of optimism.
9. **Sweetgreen (healthy food restaurant chain):** To inspire healthier communities by connecting people to real food.
10. **Honest Tea:** To create and promote great-tasting, healthy organic beverages.
11. **Patagonia:** Build the best product, cause no unnecessary harm, use business to inspire, and implement solutions to the environmental crisis.

12. **IKEA**: To create a better everyday life for the many people.
13. **Cradles to Crayons**: To provide children from birth through age twelve, living in homeless or low-income situations, with the essential items they need to thrive—at home, at school and at play.
14. **Southwest Airlines:** To connect people to what's important in their lives through friendly, reliable, low-cost air travel.
15. **CV Pharmacies:** Helping people on their path to better health
16. **REA Group**: To make the property purchasing process simple, efficient, and stress-free for people buying and selling a property.
17. **IAG Insurance:** To help people manage risk and recover from the hardship of unexpected loss.
18. **Betterment (investment company):** To empower you to make the most of your money, so you can live better.
19. **Google**: To organize the world's information and make it universally accessible and useful.
20. **Lyft (Uber alternative):** To reconnect people through transportation and bring communities together.
21. **Starbucks:** To inspire and nurture the human spirit—one person, one cup, and one neighborhood at a time.

END NOTES

CHAPTER 1

1. Wukovits, John, *Hell from the Heavens: The Epic Story of the USS Laffey and World War II's Greatest Kamikaze Attack*, Da Capo Press; Reprint edition, April 5, 2016

2. Ibid, p. 179

3. Ibid, inside book jacket cover

4. Ibid, p. 27

5. Ibid, p. 221

6. Ibid, p. 173

CHAPTER 4

1. *Employee Engagement*, Canadian Human Resources Centre article, http://www.canadahrcentre.com/solutions/employee-engagement/

2. Ibid

3. Ibid

4. *State of the American Workplace: Employee Engagement Insights for US Business Leaders*, Gallup Organization, 2016

5. Adapted from *The Business Case for a Healthy Workplace*, Industrial Accident Prevention Association, Canada, 2008

6. ibid

7. *State of the American Workplace: Employee Engagement Insights for US Business Leaders*, Gallup Organization, 2016

CHAPTER 7

1. Sinek, Simon, *Start With Why, How Great Leaders Inspire Everyone to Take Action*, Portfolio / Penguin, 2009

2. Pink, Daniel H., *Drive, The Surprising Truth About What Motivates Us*, Penguin Group USA Inc., 2009

CHAPTER 8

1. Collins, Jim, *Good To Great: Why Some Companies Make the Leap . . . And Others Don't*, Harper Business, 2001

2. Adam Leipzig, *How to Know Your Life's Purpose in Five Minutes*, https://www.youtube.com/watch?v=vVsXO9brK7M

CHAPTER 9

1. Pink, Daniel H., *Drive, The Surprising Truth About What Motivates Us*, Penguin Group USA Inc., 2009

2. Colan, Lee J., *Engaging the Hearts and Minds of all your Employees*, McGraw Hill Education, 2018, p.78

3. Heath, Chip; Heath, Dan, *The Power of Moments*, Simon and Shuster, 2017

CHAPTER 11

1. Brown, Brené, *The Gifts of Imperfection*, Hazelden Publishing, 2010, p. 19

CHAPTER 15

1. Buckingham, Marcus, *Now, Discover Your Strengths*, The Free Press, 2001, p. 54

CHAPTER 22

1. Davidson, John, *Jesse's Journey, A Canadian Story*, Timberholme Books Ltd., 2002

2. Davidson, John, *The Right Road, How Far Will You Go*, Binea Press, 2010

ACKNOWLEDGEMENTS

My publishing team at Friesen Press was key to keeping me focused and moving forward. They were top notch as they patiently guided me through the writing, editing, and publishing process. In particular, I would like to say thanks to publishing consultant Christoph Koniczek, publishing production specialist Diane Cameron, publishing specialist Liza Weppenaar, editor Laura Pratt, and designer Colin Parks (colinparks.com). Your patience, professionalism, and editorial perspective in bringing this book to completion have been awesome and much appreciated! Any errors that remain are most definitely mine. Thank you.

For sharing their wisdom, knowledge, and experience in interviews, I thank Lisa Osachoff, Scott Murakami, Trevor Campbell, and John Davidson. Your stories helped breathe additional life into the facts and practical aspects of purpose and employee engagement. You provided many different perspectives for others to build on.

My two brothers, Hal and Craig, were instrumental in helping me keep my feet on the ground by challenging me on how to apply each concept in a practical, productive way in businesses and organizations. Both of you challenged me to keep the book readable and easy to apply. You helped me see *The Three-Legged Stool* through business eyes. Craig, an additional kudo to you for the number of times you read chapters and reviewed the book in its entirety – much appreciated!

For the past year and a half, this book has permeated conversations around the table or over the phone more often that I can remember. My grown children, all business professionals in their own right, provided that intergenerational perspective that I couldn't have accomplished on my own.

At the heart of book stands Brenda, my wife and best friend ever! You have supported my long hours and continued focus on this book. You reviewed multiple versions of each chapter and I lost count of how many times you reviewed the book in its entirety. Your questions, suggestions, and consistent proofreading have been a huge part in bringing this book to life. You supported me when it seemed I couldn't get unstuck, listened to my ideas and frustrations, supported the hours the writing took away from family and business, and loved me unconditionally throughout.

ABOUT THE AUTHOR

 Dana Couillard is a highly engaging storyteller and speaker, as well as an award-winning writer. He recently received his Masters of Arts in Human Development from Saint Mary's University of Minnesota.

A professional educator and mentor for over 30 years, Dana specializes in human dynamics, thinking, and behavior at the individual and organizational levels.

His *Why*: inspiring others to create more meaningful, engaged lives, personally and at work.

His *How*: teaching new ways of perceiving and thinking.

His *What*: successfully executing individual and/or business efforts to change.

In his own words, he is driven to help others 'make change stick!'

With his brother, Hal, he previously co-authored, *Lifeworth, Finding Fulfillment Beyond Networth*, which won a 2013 Business Axiom Book Award.

Currently a fifth degree black belt, Dana is a member of the International Fudokan Traditional Karate Association and the International Traditional Karate Federation.

He lives in Lethbridge, Alberta with his wife Brenda, and they have four adult children.